THE FUTURE OF MONEY AND BANKING

A United National Non-Bank Payment System

by

Burnham P. Beckwith, Ph.D.

Published by B.P. Beckwith
656 Lytton Ave. (C430), Palo Alto, CA 94301
Price:—$8.00 postpaid

Manufactured in the United States of America
ISBN 0-9603262-7-8

PREFACE

This is not my first venture into the field of monetary and banking theory. My unpublished 1932 Ph.D. Thesis reviewed most of the 1650-1930 arguments for and against commercial banking, and my published 1935 monograph dealt with theories of the effect of such banking on the supply of physical capital. My treatise, Socialist Economy (1949) contains a 25-page chapter, "Money and Banking," and several latter books contain chapters or essays on this subject. In nearly all of these writings I implied or asserted that commercial banking, the creation and loan of bank money by banks, should be ended.

Most of the other major monetary and/or banking reforms predicted in this book have also been repeatedly discussed and/or predicted in these earlier publications of mine. For instance, in 1949 I proposed that "business enterprises should collect their debts by mailing bills to the State Bank [a monopoly] instead of to the debtor, and should receive immediate and automatic payment by the bank, instead of voluntary payment from the debtor" (p. 65), that the use of cash to make large payments should be prohibited (p. 66), and that monthly bank statements should be extensively used to detect "bribery, fraud, or crime." These ideas were restated and elaborated in Liberal Socialism (1974, pp. 59-61).

The only important new reform suggested in this book is the concentration of all demand deposits in a single new nonbank office which processes and clears all checks and check substitutes as "on us" checks. I am aware of no previous discussion of this major coming reform by any previous writer.

The next most novel feature of this book is a discussion of the comprehensive use of data on demand-deposit debits and credits as a means of detecting and preventing most forms of crime. I have discussed this reform in several previous books, but the discussion here is much more detailed and extensive than any previous one.

One other novel idea, that the state will seize all bank assets acquired by the creation of bank money, came to me as I was writing this book. Of course, this is an old socialist idea. The new and surprising element of my forecast is the claim that this act will not injure banks if they are also freed from equal demand deposit liabilities, as predicted in Ch. VI.

Although I have previously discussed nearly all of the major reforms predicted in this book, the books containing the earlier statements are out of print. Moreover, the titles of these earlier books did not suggest that they contained predictions about the future of money and banking. Therefore, I believe that it is worthwhile to revise these scattered early contributions and offer them together in a single book on the future of money and banking, with a title that properly describes its contents. The new title will help students of money and banking to find and read the predictions in this book.

CONTENTS

CHAPTER I. INTRODUCTION

Our commercial banking and monetary system is the accidental result of 200 years of largely uncontrolled competition and unplanned growth. It is a product of a competitive search for profits, not of rational planning for efficient operation in the social or national interest. Moreover, technological progress has recently made it possible to achieve highly desirable monetary reforms which were previously beyond our capacity. For both reasons, a drastic and comprehensive rationalization of our commercial banking and monetary system is almost inevitable. In this book I predict six major reforms which will probably be largely or entirely completed before 2100 A.D. These reforms will transform our monetary and banking system far more radically than all other reforms since the creation of this system.

The six major monetary and banking reforms predicted and described in this book are:

1. A long-continuing and, in time, radical concentration of demand deposits in fewer and fewer commercial banks.
2. A similar growth in the use of debit cards and electronic messages to directly debit and credit demand accounts.
3. The elimination of commercial banking, i.e., an end to the creation and destruction of bank notes and demand deposits by banks.
4. Creation of a single demand-deposit-holding agency which receives and processes all debits and credits to demand deposits.
5. Growing use of demand-deposit debit-credit data to detect and prevent crime.
6. Stabilization of the price level for consumer goods.

I have chosen to discuss these reforms because I believe that these are the most important monetary and commercial banking reforms likely to be adopted during the next 100 years. Many other less important reforms will surely be adopted, and perhaps one or two as important as the least significant in my list.

Many other writers have predicted three of the reforms listed above (1, 2, 6), but few if any have predicted the other three, by far the most important in this list. The detailed discussion of these three major coming reforms is the major contribution of this book.

2. Definition of Money and Commercial Banking

When nearly all money consisted of metal coins and paper money, it was easy to define the term money. It is far more difficult today, when depositors can write checks on demand deposits, savings deposits, brokerage accounts, and credits granted by other kinds of firms. But it is still vital to define money so as to include any means of payment which is both legal tender and generally accepted by business men. Demand deposits are still by far the most important form of money in the U.S. In some European countries, bank notes are more widely used than checks and demand deposits, but both are created by banks, and may therefore properly be called bank money. In time, all such bank money will be replaced by government-created paper money, most of which will serve as 100% reserves behind demand deposits.

I define commercial banking as the creation, holding, and transfer, from one account to another, of demand deposits. Commercial banks now perform many other functions, but I only discuss their creation and handling of demand deposits, the most important form of money in most advanced countries.

The most significant single fact about commercial banks is that they create over 80% of the demand deposits they hold. Most Americans are probably still unaware that banks create money. Indeed, recognition of this fact by economists and bankers became general only in this century, and many still deny it. For instance, Professor Edwin Cannan, who taught banking theory at the University of London, rejected it as late as 1928. He taught that commercial banks function like hat check stands, which clearly do not create hats.

Commercial banks create new money in the form of new demand deposits when they credit borrowers with new demand deposits. It is often claimed that such banks merely loan out "idle" money deposited in them. This can happen, but in the vast majority of cases they retain old deposits, and make loans by creating new, fictitious deposits in the names of the borrowers. Moreover, the money in old deposits is rarely idle. The depositors continue to spend it by writing checks on it. Idle funds are deposited in savings banks or accounts, not in commercial banks. These points will be elaborated in Chapter IV.

In the U.S. some 200 billion payments were made in 1985, about 72% in cash. The average cash payment was close to $25, and the total about 2.8 trillion (Berger, 18). The cost of printing, replacing, and handling cash has been estimated at $3 billion a year, most of which was paid by the federal government (Bender, 11). However, this estimate probably does not include real costs incurred by the public —theft, burglary, loss, destruction, counting, spending on wallets, etc.

About 54 billion checks and credit-card slips were used to make total payments of some $46 trillion, a total 15 times as large as the total for cash payments. Thus, in the U.S., the theory of money, including the theory of price level control, is largely the theory of control over the quantity of demand deposits.

In the last decade many banks, brokers, retail stores, trust companies, S & Ls, etc., which were never listed as commercial banks, have begun to accept demand deposits and checks drawn on these deposits. They have become commmercial banks by definition. This has greatly increased the need for reform of commercial banking. It has markedly raised the average cost of processing bank checks, has increased the number and value of bank failures, and has greatly increased the difficulty and cost of government control over banks and the quantity of money in circulation.

3. Is Scientific Prediction Possible?

Many critics of futurism have asserted that it is impossible to predict future social changes because men have freedom of will, because future scientific breakthroughs are unpredictable, because the causation of social changes is extremely complex and little understood, and for other reasons. Since I have discussed these and other objections to scientific futurism in previous books—including The Next 500 Years (1967) and Ideas About the Future (1984, 1986)—I shall not do so again here. In these earlier books I also recorded many notable successes in scientific prediction of future social trends.

It is noteworthy that the harshest critics of scientific futurism do not hesitate to plan their own future on the basis of many of their own predictions, often unconscious or unstated, about future events and trends. Indeed, their lives would be uncontrollable if they could not predict the behavior of other people.

In Chapter I, "The Nature of Scientific Prediction," in The Next 500 Years (1967), I discussed 12 methods of scientific prediction, and the arguments for and against the possibility of such prediction. I also explained which kinds of prediction are more, or less, likely to be reliable. I do not think it necessary to restate that chapter here. However, I shall now explain which methods of prediction are most frequently used in this book.

All scientific futurists rely heavily on the projection of recent social trends into the future, and such projection is used in this book. It is never certain that a past trend will continue into future, but it is usually very probable. The older and more stable the trend, the safer it is to project it into the future, especially when the main conditions responsible for it appear likely to continue.

The chief unusual method of prediction used here is the theory that one can determine how a problem will be solved by determining the best method of solution, and then predicting its adoption. This was the method of prediction used by Condorcet and other pioneer neo-Malthusians when they predicted the eventual general adoption of artificial birth control, long before statistics on such birth control were available. Many other great social reforms—abolition of slavery, free public education, free health care, votes for women, etc.—were successfully predicted by pioneer futurists long before supporting statistical data were available. Jacques Ellul, the French sociologist, has summarized this method briefly in his claim that "there is only one best technological solution for any social problem, and that therefore every society will eventually adopt all such best solutions." This method of prediction is most useful and reliable in the most advanced countries, where people are the best educated and the most accustomed to technological arguments and change. However, it is not useful in predicting the rate of progress towards these reforms. For the latter, we need reliable statistics on past trends in relevant public and expert opinion.

CHAPTER II. THE TREND TOWARDS CONCENTRATION

1. Concentration of Bank Assets

The most easily predictable and highly probable major future trnd in commercial banking during the next 100 years is a long-continuing further concentration of demand deposits in fewer and larger banks. This long-run trend will include, or be the result of three constituent trends: (1) the merger of formerly independent banks into larger units, (2) the merger and growth of chain banks and bank-holding companies, and (3) the failure of many small-town banks, due to the continuing movement of population from rural to urban areas. In 1980 there were about 15,000 independent commercial banks in the U.S. By 2050 A.D. the number will probably be less than 1000, and 90% of all bank assets will be held by less than 10 firms. By the year 2100, all demand deposits will be held by a single firm, but, as explained in Chapter VI, it will not be a bank.

A significant temporary reversal of this long-run trend may now be occurring because the U.S. government has recently (1980, 1982), for the first time, allowed most savings banks, brokers, and other firms, to hold demand deposits transferable by check. (This reversal will be discussed later in this chapter.) It will take at least a decade to determine the effect of these changes on bank concentration, but in any case, the long-run concentration trend will soon re-appear or continue. There are several good reasons for the past existence and the probable future continuance of this trend.

2. The Causes of this Concentration

The first and most important reason for the concentration of demand deposits in fewer and ever larger banks is that, other factors being equal, every increase in the size of a commercial bank reduces its operating costs per unit of service.

(1) Economies of Scale and Scope

The larger the bank, the more feasible is an ever more intensive division of labor among bank employees and office equipment. A giant bank can employ officers who specialize in making loans to a single industry, which reduces loan risks. A small bank cannot practice such a division of labor.

In recent years engineers have created many new and more expensive office machines—computers, check-processors, work stations, etc.—and small banks cannot use all such equipment economically because their volume of business is not large enough to permit full use of it. Moreover, larger, ever more specialized and expensive machines will be designed for use in the largest banks.

Every increase in the size of a bank also enables it to buy office supplies and equipment at lower prices because it can buy them in larger quantities. And it can borrow money more cheaply, both because it borrows larger sums and because it has a higher credit rating.

Since a large bank makes more loans to more customers, it can achieve a greater diversification of risk. A small bank usually loans money largely to local business men, all of whom may be seriously hurt by a local catastrophe or economic decline. A giant bank can make loans to customers in many industries throughout the nation. And it will attract the largest firms, the safest risks, as borrowers because it can make the largest loans at the lowest interest rates.

Every increase in the size of the region served by a bank with branches enables it to better serve all of its depositors because it enables every customer to make deposits and cash checks throughout a larger area. From the standpoint of bank customers, an ideal bank would have branches in every town and shopping district in both his country and all other countries. No U.S. bank can provide such service today.

The larger the home bank the greater the number of services it can perform for its customers—including trust services, the sale of insurance and securities, investment counseling, tax advice, etc. And it can afford to hire more competent employees to provide such services. Moreover, the provision of such services helps to attract new depositors and hold on to old ones.

Every merger of two or more banks in the same city makes local advertising more effective and/or cheaper, and reduces the time and money bank employees spend going to and from work. It also gives customers a wider choice of bank offices to serve them.

Moreover, every bank merger increases the number of "on us" checks, which are much cheaper to handle than other checks. As explained in Chapter VI, this advantage alone is so great that it will eventually result in a concentration of all demand deposits in a single agency, where all checks will be "on us."

It is noteworthy that in the banking industry, as in nearly all other industries, the large firms pay higher wage rates and offer more nonwage benefits —pensions, health insurance, day care for the children of workers, etc.—than do the small firms. For instance, 82% of U.S. large firms (500+ workers) offer pensions to workers, but only 23% of small firms (1-99 workers) do so (S.F.Chronicle, 5-11-87). The large firms can afford to treat their workers better, and still grow faster, only because of economies of scale and scope. For the same reason, they can afford to treat their depositors and borrowers better, and that is one of the chief reasons they are growing faster than small banks.

The higher wages paid by big banks and the superior service they give customers are the result of, and evidence of, significant economies in scale and scope, but they have been ignored by most researchers on such economies. Indeed the increase in wage and benefit costs can be used to suggest that the economies of scale are small or nonexistent.

Some economists have denied that big U.S. commercial banks enjoy significant economies of scale when they grow larger. But the fact that small banks have always fought bitterly to minimize competition from big banks clearly implies that the big banks are more efficient. And the fact that the failure rate among small banks is much higher than that among big banks supports the same conclusion.

Orthodox economists have a strong incentive to deny economies of scale, because, when such economies exist, competition tends to be replaced by monopoly, and the entire orthodox theory of price determination in competitive markets becomes false or obsolete.

The most recent and most authoritative study of economies of scale is that published by Colin Lawrence and R. P. Shay in 1986. They discovered previously unreported evidence of such economies.

Using a sample of banks that participated in the Federal Reserve System's functional cost analysis for the years 1979-82, they found evidence of economies of scale in 3 of 4 quartiles (1, 2, and 4) of banks arrayed by asset size. It is significant that these economies continued among the largest banks.

The earnings of large banks are not only larger per dollar of capital but also grow faster and/or are more secure. As a result, stock market values per dollar of bank earnings are usually much higher for large banks than for small banks. For instance, in California, for 17 banks that were sold in 1986, the PE ratio for the larger banks (22.2) was 50% above that for the smaller banks (S.F.Chron., 4-11-87, p. 52).

(2) Other Reasons Why Banks Favor Growth in Size

Even if there are no substantial economies of scale in the banking industry, many senior bank executives believe that such economies are substantial, and this is one of the chief reasons most such executives strive constantly to increase the size of their bank. Another important reason is that every increase in bank size increases the prestige, the salary, and the economic influence of the chief executives. Finally, most bank presidents favor mergers because they believe that a merger with a competitor will reduce the intensity of competition and enable their bank to reduce spending on advertising and sales effort, and earn higher profits. For the same reason, most bank executives strive constantly to prevent the creation of new banks which will compete with them.

(3) European Trends

Another reason for predicting continued concentration of U.S. demand deposits in the hands of ever fewer and larger banks is that this trend has already gone much further in other advanced countries. The U.K. has only about 12 commercial banks, Canada less than 10. The 5 largest U.K. banks have over 10,000 branches, and hold 75% of all demand deposits. Major social trends are similar in all advanced countries because the same, or very similar, causal conditions exist in each of them. One nation may fall behind the others in certain trends, but such lags are usually offset by later spurts. Moreover, the chief reason for the U.S. lag in concentration of demand deposits, legal restriction of chain banking, will soon disappear.

(4) Laws Against Concentration Will Weaken

The economies of scale are so well-known that small U.S. banks have always sought, and have usually obtained, strong legal protection against competition with chain banks and large-city banks. Like most other business men, bankers often and loudly preach the virtues of free competition, especially among job seekers, but during office hours they strive constantly to reduce competition in their own home town and industry.

As a result of vigorous political activity by small-town bankers, most state governments had prohibited branch banking by state-chartered banks before 1900. In 1926, by the McFadden Act, the U.S. Congress forbade all banks to open offices outside their home states, and denied national banks the right to open branches within a state unless the state banks were allowed to do so. And other federal legislation imposed the same restrictions on bank-holding companies in 1956.

California was long one of the few states that permitted intrastate chain banking, and, as a result, the Bank of America, the largest chain bank in California, became for some years the largest bank in the the U.S. and the world.

i. Recent Changes in State Laws

In recent years, state laws protecting small banks against competition from large banks have been increasingly revised or repealed, to allow more and more of such competition. By April, 1986, 37 states and the District of Columbia had approved some form of intrastate chain banking and/or interstate banking. Nine states had allowed all out-of-state banks to establish branches, 18 had "trigger dates" to permit such competition, and the rest had allowed all banks in some nearby states to compete with local banks. Only a third of the states still prohibited all chain banking.

ii. The Decline of Small-Bank Political Power

The recent revisions and repeals of state laws against chain banking were not due to a sudden general understanding of the economies of scale and the increase in social welfare achievable by the growth of chain banking systems and giant big-city banks. The owners of small banks were always fully aware of these economies. That is why they sought and secured legal protection from competition from chain banks. The real reason for the recent major reduction in such protection is that small-town bankers and their local political allies have long been losing their once great and undue political influence due to an immense and still-continuing movement of population from farms and small towns to metropolitan areas.

Technological progress in agriculture has made it possible for one farmer to produce more than ten farmers produced in 1864, the year our federal government prohibited interstate banking. Moreover, new laws and court decisions have drastically reduced the once inordinate political representation of the rural population in state legislatures. For instance, the "one man one vote" decision of the U.S. Supreme Court compelled all states to base reprsentation in state legislatures on population, not acreage. Before that decision, every small cow-county in California elected the same number of senators (one) as the great cities of Los Angeles and San Francisco. Unfortunately, agricultural states like Nevada (population one million) still elect the same number of U.S. senators as California (population 25 million) which is the major reason why Congress still prohibits interstate banking.

Technolgical progress in agriculture has also resulted in almost continuous overproduction of farm products and in bankruptcy of many farmers and farm town banks. This has further reduced the political power of small-town bankers, and will long continue to do so. For such reasons, Colin and Shay recently (1985) concluded that "The potent political power of small banks...will not be strong enough to offset the overpowering appeal of the emerging bank supermarkets on a regional or national basis" (p. 9).

Fortunately, the big chain banks have learned from experience that the best way to expand into new areas is to buy out small-bank stockholders. Since such stockholders have usually received generous prices for stock previously hard to sell, they are rapidly becoming reconciled to the probable future rise of national chain banking. Chain banks can afford to offer generous and tempting bids for small banks because they know that these banks will become much more profitable when operated as branches of chain banks. It is highly probable, therefore, that most small U.S. banks which do not fail in the meantime will be purchased by large banks before 2050 A.D.

Moreover, the continued concentration of agriculture in fewer and more efficient farms will cause many small-town banks to fail or reduce their dividends, and this will help to persuade many stockholders in such banks to sell their stock to chain banks.

(5) The Elimination of State Banks

The American banking system has been a dual system since 1865 when Congress authorized federal licensing of a new class of banks, called national banks, to compete with the state banks, licensed and and regulated by state governments.

It is generally recognized that such a dual system is inherently less efficient and more costly than a one-class system would be. Competition between the two classes of banks has resulted in one relaxation of standards after another, which has notably increased the number of bank failures. Competition between banks regulated by different states has had similar harmful effects. Moreover, customary government regulation is much less efficient and much more costly than it need be because all 50 states and the federal government must maintain separate regulatory agencies. And the mere existence of 51 separate systems of banking laws and bank-regulating agencies makes it more difficult for depositors and borrowers, who often move from state to state or who do business in two or more states, to learn of the banking laws and regulations which control their bank and its services to them.

The U.S. badly needs a single uniform national system of banks and banking laws. The chief opponents of this much-needed reform are the state banks, especially snall-town state banks, who believe they now benefit from relatively lax state regulation, and states-right ideologues, who have opposed most federal social reforms since 1865. Fortunately, for reasons already given, the political power of small-town bankers and conservative states-right politicians has been declining steadily since 1860, and will continue to decline indefinitely. Thus, I can confidently predict the eventual creation of a one-class national banking system, but there is little trend data on which to base a prediction on how soon this will occur. In this field, as in many others, we badly need more data on trends in both public and and expert public opinion.

I have not discussed this prediction as a major one in this book because it has been ably discussed by other writers, and is much less significant than any of the six major future monetary reforms I do feature.

The elimination of 50 state banking systems will facilitate the continuing concentration of commercial bank assets in ever fewer hands because the state banking officials have usually opposed such concentration.

(6) Objections to the Concentration Trend

The chief nonparochial objection to the growth of concentration in banking is that it may result in a decrease in competition among banks and, therefore, higher profits for bankers. However, two forms of concentration—the expansion of chain banking and the spread of interstate banking—probably increase competition because they increase the number of competitors in most cities. For instance, when the big New York banks are allowed to open branches in large California cities, competition among banks there will increase. That is why most California banks have long opposed the legalization of interstate banking.

It has also been argued that continued concentration of bank assets in ever fewer banks will result in continued concentration of economic and, therefore, political power in ever fewer hands. But concentration of economic and political power can and will be limited by other means, means less costly than the restriction of bank concentration. For instance, public financing of political campaigns will continue to increase indefinitely, and many measures to reduce campaign costs—such as requiring the media to give free time and space to candidates—will be adopted.

A third argument against concentration of commercial banking is that it will drive many small-town banks out of business and will speed up the movement of wealth, jobs, and population from small towns to larger towns and cities. This charge is probably justified. However, the continued decline of American small towns is probably inevitable because employment in agriculture will long continue to decline, and because most other industries can operate more efficiently in large towns and cities than in small towns.

3. Some Recent Law Changes and Bank Mergers

In 1982 a new federal law allowed bank-holding companies to buy failing savings and loan companies. In 1982, Citicorp bought a failing S and L in California, and renamed it Citicorp Savings. Later it purchased S and Ls in Florida and Illinois. These S and Ls can now hold demand deposits subject to transfer by check or EFT. In December, 1986, about 20% of all U.S. S and Ls were still in trouble, so the field for purchase of S and Ls was still wide.

An 1985 Supreme Court decision approved the formation of "regional banking compacts" which permit mergers between banks within a specified region, but exclude mergers with banks outside the region.

In 1985 Citicorp induced the Maryland legislature to grant it full commercial banking privileges in return for promising to hire 1,000 workers for a new credit-card-processing plant in Hagerstown, in a depressed area.

In 1986 the State government of California passed a law authorizing California banks to operate in several other western states, starting in June, 1987, and nationwide in 1991. In 1986, Wells Fargo & Co. purchased the Crocker National Corp., thereby achieving the largest bank merger in U.S. history. In the same year, First Interstate, the ninth-largest U.S. bank, offered to buy the Bank of America, once the largest U.S. bank. When this offer was made, Interstate already had subsidiary banks in 12 Western states, and affiliates in 6 states.

Los Angeles-based Security Pacific Corporation, the sixth-largest U.S. bank-holding company, purchased the third-largest Arizona commmercial bank in 1986, and had tentatively agreed to acquire the Oregon Bank and the Nevada National Bank. And several other California banks were active in the bank merger movement (SFC, 11-2-86, p. D2).

The 1986 decline in oil prices weakened Texas banks so that 23 failed and the State of Texas quickly passed emergency legislation allowing out-of-state banks to acquire Texas banks.

In December, 1986, Chemical New York Corporation, the sixth-largest U.S. bank-holding company, announced that it would acquire Texas Commerce Bankshares for $1.2 billion, the largest bank merger in U.S. history. It created a new company with some $75 billion in assets.

The day after the announcement of the Chemical acquisition, Republic Bank and Inter-First, the 2nd and 3rd largest Texas banks, announced that they would merge, creating the 12th largest U.S. bank. Republic Bank reported that the merger would result in a cut in the workforce of 3000, or 18%, and would result in the closing of 109 overlapping branches.

In 1986 Oregon legalized regional interstate banking and Washington legalized national interstate banking. Within less than a year, 8 local banks had been sold to out-of-state banks, and 2 to intrastate banks. In March, 1987, the Security Pacific Corporation, a giant California bank-holding company, gained control of the Seattle-based Rainier Bancorp through an exchange of assets valued at about $1.15 billion, making the merger the second largest ever U.S. bank merger. Security also purchased two small Washington banks, and the Oregon Bank of Portland ($832 million deposits).

The Key Corporation, an upstate N.Y. bank-holding firm (with $9.1 billion in assets and units in N.Y., Maine, and Alaska) bought five Oregon-Washington banks, including PacWest ($735 million in assets) and the Seattle Trust and Savings Bank, Washington's second largest with 25 branches. It planned to purchase the First Northwest Bancorp of Seattle.

In December, 1986, First Nationwide, the seventh largest U.S. savings and loan bank ($15 billion) took over the St. Louis Federal Savings and Loan Association, a $1 billion bank with 25 offices, in exchange for the right to expand into Illinois, Michigan, and New Jersey, as well as Missouri. Before the takeover, it already had 231 branches in seven states: California, New York, Florida, Hawaii, Ohio, and Colorado. Its announced goal was to operate in all of the 23 most populous U.S. states (S.F.Chronicle, 12-29-86). First Nationwide acquired the St. Louis bank and expansion rights under a bidding process conducted by the Federal Savings and Loan Insurance Corporation. Many more such auctions of troubled banks are likely.

Eight days after its purchase of the St. Louis Federal S and L, Interstate announced that it had purchased the Lincoln Federal Savings and Loan Association of Louisville ($471 million in assets, 22 branches). This deal gave Interstate the right to operate in three more states (Kentucky, Virginia, and Maryland). The president of Interstate reported that additional mergers in 1986 might increase Interstate assets by 50%.

In March, 1987, the Fleet Financial Group of Providence, R.I., announced that it will acquire

Norstar Bancorp of Albany, N.Y., for nearly $1.3 billion in stock, the highest price ever paid for a bank in the U.S. The deal tops the $1.2 billion takeover of Texas Commerce Bankshares by Chemical Bank of New York as the most expensive bank merger ever. The resulting institution will have $23 billion in assets, making it the 21st-largest banking organization in the U.S. The new company will be called Fleet-Norstar Financial Group, Inc.

In 1985, New York's Chase Manhattan, the third-largest U.S. bank, began to do some business in Ohio and Maryland by buying troubled savings banks. Citicorp used the same method to get into California, Illinois, and Florida.

Manufacturers Hanover, a great New York City bank, purchased CIT Corporation, thereby acquiring 630 consumer-loan offices in 43 states.

Moreover, large banks have learned how to circumvent or evade the federal law against interstate banking by establishing out-of-state financial offices which provide many banking services but omit one or two services which, according to the federal law, would qualify these branches as commercial banks. For instance, they may make loans but refuse to accept demand deposits, or vice versa. The ownership of such so-called "nonbanks" by out-of-state commercial banks was approved by the U.S. Supreme Court on April 20, 1987.

Citicorp, the largest U.S. bank, $186 billion in deposits, already owns full-service banks in 9 states and D.C., and claims 20% of all U.S. families among its customers. Banc One, a Columbus, Ohio, holding company with $12 billion in assets, has gone after 13 banks in Indiana, Kentucky, Michigan, and Wisconsin. NCNB, a Charlotte, N.C., bank, has acquired 8 banks in South Carolina, Georgia, and Florida, and has announced plans to buy banks in Maryland and Virginia. By November, 1986, almost 100 banks had been sold to out-of-state banks, and another 100 were in the works.

It is noteworthy that nearly all of these bank mergers occurred in the two years 1985 and 1986, almost immediately after anti-merger laws were repealed. This implies that the desire for merger is very strong and will result in many more mergers.

4. Data on the Growth of Branch Banking, 1900-80

Concentration of deposits and capital in the commercial banking industry has been largely achieved in all advanced countries by the expansion of branch banking. Although U.S. GNP grew by about 100% between 1930 and 1980, the number of independent U.S. commercial banks fell by 38%, but the number of bank branches grew by about 700%.

The following table shows that the number of commercial bank branches grew rapidly and continuously from 119 in 1900 to 41,902 in 1980, and the number doubled in each decade except from 1930-40, the decade of the Great Depression. Obviously such a rate of growth cannot continue, but the assets per bank can continue to grow at a very high rate.

	Commercial Banks with Branches	No. of Branches	No. of Commercial Banks
1900	87	119	12,427
1910	292	548	24,514
1920	530	1,281	30,291
1930	751	3,522	23,679
1940	959	3,531	14,532
1950	1,241	4,721	14,146
1960	2,329	10,216	13,508
1970	3,994	21,424	13,690
1980		41,902	14,836

Source: _HSUS_, Vol. 2 (1975), pp. 1036-7 and pp. 1621-22 Series X731-740, X588-609

In 1984 some 500 insured commercial banks with assets of more than $0.5 billion apiece made up only 3.3% of all commercial banks but held 63.2% of all insured commercial bank assets in the U.S. (SAUS, 1986, p. 492). And among the 500, the 100 largest controlled over half of all commercial bank assets. The smallest 10,000 such banks held only about 10% of assets. Clearly these 10,000 are superfluous. They will be rapidly bought out or driven out of business soon after the larger banks are allowed to compete with or buy them. I predict that nearly all of them will disappear within 60 years, and that, by the year 2050, the U.S. will have less than 100 commercial banks. Soon thereafter, if not before, the U.S. government will concentrate all demand deposits in a single check-clearing agency, for reasons given in Chapter VI.

5. Some Supporting Forecasts

Paul Volcker, long-time chairman of the Federal Reserve Board, has recommended that laws against interstate banking be repealed. William Isaac, former chairman of the Federal Deposit Insurance Corporation, has predicted that American banking will be dominated by a few megafirms.

In a recent Fortune article (10-27-86), Duane Hansen forecast that, "By the early 1990s there may be as few as 30 nationwide banks that will control 50% of all deposits in the U.S."

James Christian, chief economist of the U.S. League of savings institutions, has called the trend to interstate banking "Irresistable, irreversible." In an April, 1987, article in U.S. Banker Alan Wade quoted Christian's strong words with approval, and asserted that this view was held by most American bankers.

John Heimann, former Controller of the Currency, has forecast a future in which "25 to 50 financial institutions, not all of them banks, will dominate the financial services industry worldwide" (Mayer, 372). Many other bankers and economists have come to similar conclusions. The only original feature of my prediction is that I predict a complete integration of the function of holding demand deposits and clear-demand deposits and debits. This distinctive feature of my prediction on concentration is important enough to be treated as a separate major prediction, and is treated as such in Chapter VI.

6. The Recent Temporary Deconcentration of Demand Deposits

My chief thesis in this chapter is that demand deposits will continue to be concentrated in ever fewer and larger banks. This is an old trend. However, it has been, or will be temporarily reversed by a recent one-time event, the conversion of many savings accounts into demand accounts, i.e., into accounts against which checks can be written. This one-time change greatly increased the quantity of money because any account on which checks can be drawn is money, and also reduced the concentration of demand deposits in large banks.

Until about 1980, nearly all checks on U.S. banks were used to transfer demand accounts in commercial banks, and the national total of demand deposits was loosely and indirectly controlled by the Federal Reserve System. But, since 1980, S and Ls and some other financial firms have been permitted to grant the use of checks to their customers. This radical reform turned savings deposits into demand deposits. Moreover, about the same time, the customers of stock brokers were allowed to write checks against deposits and securities held by brokers. Most such securities are highly liquid assets because they can be sold easily and quickly on security exchanges. Since the total value of liquid securities held by brokers is probably over $500 billion, this reform also permitted an enormous increase in the quantity of money in use.

There seems to be no logical limit to this process of monetizing assets not previously used as money or as a basis for credit balances. Many pioneer promoters of commercial banks advocated the creation of land banks which could monetize land by issuing bank notes backed by land. In fact, the securities of mortgage investment firms can now be monetized by depositing them in a security brokerage firm.

Since the monetization of savings deposits and deposited securities is so recent, it is impossible to predict the effect upon U.S. price levels, and upon the concentration of demand deposits, but it may be very great, and any inflationary effects will increase the need for concentrating control over the quantity of money in the hands of a single national agency which will use this control to stabilize price levels and/or the rate of national economic growth.

The changes noted above increased greatly the number of commercial banks. However, I predict that the long-run decline in the number of such banks will soon re-appear, and will continue for many decades, until ended by the prohibition of all commercial banking.

The recent temporary expansion of commercial banking occurred largely because, beginning in 1980, the U.S. government allowed commercial banks to pay interest on demand deposits. This prompted the savings banks and other financial institutions to begin to treat savings accounts, which had long earned interest, as demand deposits, in order to enable them to compete with commercial banks which paid interest on demand deposits.

Both new policies are very uneconomic. Funds placed in savings deposits should earn interest because saving or abstinence is painful and should be rewarded. But when a depositor can continue to spend the funds he has deposited, he has not saved, i.e., abstained from consumption. He has merely exchanged one form of money for another, and therefore he should not be paid interest on his deposit. Rather, for reasons explained in Chapter VII, he should pay fees for the services he receives. Thus, the new bank policies, allowing the continued spending of saved funds and paying interest on demand deposits, are both illogical and uneconomic. Therefore, both practices will eventually be prohibited. But I cannot predict how soon these reforms will occur.

CHAPTER III. MORE USE OF DIRECT EFT

1. My Second Prediction

My second major prediction concerning the future evolution of money and banking in the U.S., and in all other advanced countries, is that there will occur a rapid and great increase in the use of direct electronic debiting and crediting of demand accounts, i.e., of direct electronic fund transfer, or to be brief, of direct EFT. In 1985, less than 2% of U.S. demand-deposit debits and credits were made by direct EFT (White, p. 23). I predict that this figure will rise to about 40% by 2040, and above 90% by 2100 A.D.

(1) Two Parts of this Prediction

My forecast includes two distinct and separate changes: (1) the replacement of payment by check with payment by electronic fund transfer (EFT), and (2) adoption of the practice of sending bills and payments <u>directly</u> to the relevant demand-deposit holding agency, instead of sending them to the debtor or creditor. This second reform could easily be adopted before the first is adopted. In other words, bills and checks, as well as EFT orders, can be sent directly to relevant banks, and debited or credited to demand accounts, thus speeding up payment and greatly reducing payment costs. But the use of wire EFT payment requires direct debiting and crediting to demand deposits.

When predicting the future of major social trends, futurists have usually grossly overestimated the rate of change. Many early writers on the growth of electronic banking predicted that this growth would be far more rapid than it has actually been. They ignored, or radically underestimated, the difficulty of persuading 15,000 commercial banks and their millions of depositors to agree on and adopt new methods of behavior. If compared with most previous predictions, my estimate of the future rate of expansion of EFT is very conservative. Nevertheless, the final result will be a great and radical change in the way depositors debit and credit their demand deposits.

(2) Two Types of EFT

Some writers distinguish between electronic transmission of batches of EFT orders and the transmission of individual EFT orders by wire. When batch EFT is used, many transfer orders are assembled in a single message, or on an electronic tape, and transmission of the composite message or tape may be postponed until a later hour, usually during night time, when transmission charges are lower. Wire transfers transmit a single debit or credit, go through instantly, and permit immediate verification. They have been used chiefly to shift large funds between banks, and banks charge $10 or more per wire. This high cost has persuaded some writers that the use of wire transfers to pay for retail purchases will long be uneconomic. This conclusion is questionable because wire transmission costs will probably fall by over 95% when this means of payment is generally used by retail customers. Moreover, technological progress will continue to reduce wire transmission costs for any volume of traffic. I predict that, by 2050 A.D., all urgent EFT orders will be by wire. However, today nearly all U.S. EFT orders are transmitted in batches through automated clearing houses (ACHs), and batch EFT may always be used for most nonurgent payments.

Many brokerage offices now contain equipment which customers and visitors can use to wire the New York Stock Exchange, free of charge, to obtain current security prices. The fact that such service is provided without charge implies that wire use is already very cheap, even during hours of peak use.

Since payment by wire is as electronic as payment by EFT, I shall use EFT to cover both methods of payment.

(3) How Direct EFT Differs from Payment by Check

The customary method of paying bills by check has long required eight different actions: (1) the preparation of a bill or invoice by a creditor, (2) its delivery to the debtor, usually by mail, (3) the reaction of the debtor to receipt of the bill, including checking the bill against his records, (4) writing a check for the amount specified, and mailing it to the creditor, usually from one to 31 days after his receipt of the bill, (5) the receipt and review of the check by the creditor, (6) his submission of it to his bank, usually different from the bank of the debtor, (7) collection of the check by the creditor's bank, which normally requires processing of the check by two to ten banks, clearing houses, and other agencies, and (8) the debiting of the check to the demand deposit of the check-writer.

The substitution of direct EFT payment for check payment will completely eliminate four of these steps or actions (2, 4, 5, 6), and will simplify and/or speed up steps 7 and 8. When a direct EFT payment is made, the creditor sends his bill directly to the debtor's bank, where it is immediately debited to the debtor's demand deposit and credited to the creditor's demand account or that of his bank. When wire EFT is used, if the debtor's account is not large enough to cover the bill, the creditor is instantly notified, and can halt any uncompleted delivery of goods. All debits and credits due to direct EFT payment are reported in periodic bank statements which enable both debtors and creditors to check such debits and credits, and to complain of any errors. The creation of a single national demand-deposit and payment clearing monopoly, (PCA), predicted later, will greatly facilitate such direct payment to payee's bank because, after this reform, all payees and payors will have their demand deposits in the same office.

When checks are used to pay for goods and services, they are normally returned to bank customers with the monthly bank statements, and can be used as evidence of payment. When direct debiting of debtors' demand accounts replaces payment by check, debtors will be able to use the debits reported in their bank or payment statements as proof of payment.

(4) Direct EFT Is Not a New Idea

Direct payment to payees' bank accounts is not a new, untried idea. It has been common in Western Europe for many years. In 1960 both the American Bankers' Association and the Federal Reserve System recommended the use of direct EFT. And in 1974 the U.S. government began to make social security payments directly to payees' banks. This eliminates both loss of checks in transit and theft of checks after receipt. It saves payees the cost and inconvenience of a trip to the bank, or of any other effort required to deposit checks, and it assures faster crediting of payees' accounts. A growing number of U.S. firms have begun to pay wages and salaries directly to employees' bank accounts. I predict that by 2050 nearly all wage, dividend, and interest payments will be so paid.

According to Flannery and Jaffe (p. 63), "The concept of an electrified money system dates at least to 1954, when two M.I.T. professors [R.H. Gregory and H. Jacobs] suggested that the best means of handling the pressing problem of increasing paper flows in the banking system was simply to computerize the whole process and eliminate paper altogether." This was one of the most original and brilliant insights in the history of political economy. If Gregory and Jacobs were the first to publish this theory, they deserve far more recognition than they have so far received. But I suspect that further research may reveal earlier statements of this theory. The theory is of extraordinary importance because its application will revolutionize monetary and banking behavior, and will increase U.S. GNP by over $40 billion a year. In spite of its great importance, the idea of electronic payment is mentioned in very few currently used university texts on the principles of economics or on money and/or banking.

2. Partial Use of Direct EFT

It is possible to take one or more steps toward the full adoption of direct EFT without adopting all of it. Creditors can send bills to their debtors' banks by mail instead of by wire, which makes instant verification of payment impossible. Debtors can send checks directly to creditors' banks. Employers can directly deduct agreed sums from pay checks, and the deducted sums can be forwarded electronically by the employer to the charity, the insurance company, the public utility, etc., specified by the worker. Banks also can directly deduct agreed sums each month from the demand deposits of their depositors, and can then, directly or indirectly, credit them to the accounts of the agreed recipients. These agreements may remain in force for many months. They assure repeated payment of routine bills without any action of the depositor after the agreement has been signed. All such partial measures reduce payment costs, but not nearly as much as complete use of direct EFT can do.

The use of automatic teller machines (ATMs) to withdraw cash from deposits is a step towards full use of direct EFT because it debits deposits directly. And employers can use EFT to pay wages without using EFT for other payments. Still other forms of partial use of EFT are possible.

Such partial use of EFT is already common in the US., and will continue to become more common for decades. It will help to convince businessmen and the public of the advantages of full use of EFT by all firms and individuals.

The town of Northhampton in England has perhaps gone further than any U.S. city towards the achievement of cashless shopping by means of EFT. Over 100 local shops allow customers to use bank debit cards to purchase goods up to $6,000 in value. The system was installed in 1985, and has reduced supermarket check-out time to less than 20 seconds. Retailers pay a quarterly rental fee for EFT equipment, and charge customers a small fee on each purchase. The system was installed by the Anglia Building Society.

Some 44 countries around the world have adopted the giro method of payment which enables holders of post-office demand deposits to instruct the post office to debit their deposit and credit that of another depositor. This saves both the cost of sending a check to the creditor and the cost to the creditor of processing and debiting the check. Moreover, all payment orders go through one central office, and are as cheap to handle as checks "on us." For these reasons, payment by giro is much less costly than payment by check.

3. The Growing Use of Bank Money

Before the year 1700, nearly all payments were made with money coined or printed by the state. Since then the use of bank money—demand deposits and bank notes—has grown much faster than the use of state money in all countries, especially in the most advanced countries. In California, 95% of all households now have checking accounts. In the U.S. about 80% in value of all payments are made with bank money. These proportions will probably continue to grow as long as banks are allowed to create bank money. The rising use of EFT will speed up this trend because it will reduce the cost of using bank money.

It is obvious that banks print bank notes and loan them to borrowers, but many people are still unaware that banks create money when they create additional demand deposits out of thin air, and loan or invest them. Such deposits are money because they are an addition to the total supply of means of payment.

Since 1860 the use of demand-deposit debits and credits to make payments in the U.S. has grown much faster than the use of bank notes. Today, the total annual value of payments by check ($20 trillion) is over 16 times that paid by bank note.

The use of checks has grown much faster than the use of banknotes and coins because it is usually much cheaper, safer, and more convenient to send a check through the mail than to send cash by mail, or to deliver it in person. If one keeps or carries large sums of cash, they may be lost or stolen, and stolen checks are much harder to spend than stolen currency. Moreover, checks can be written for the exact amount required, and they serve as receipts when returned to the payee or entered in his bank account.

These and other private advantages of the use of bank checks are well known. In addition, there are very important social advantages. As explained later, the use of checks leaves bank records which can be used, and increasingly will be used, by government agencies to enforce payment of taxes and to prevent and detect all crimes involving the theft or payment of money. For this reason, the U.S. government will increasingly limit the use of cash to make large payments. By 2100 A.D., such use will be prohibited. This will compel people to make all large payments by check or check substitute.

Another and newer reason why the use of demand-deposit debits and credits to make payments has been growing is that bankers and other business men have recently learned that it is much cheaper to make demand-deposit debits and credits by means of electronic orders than by using checks. As explained later, the average full social cost of using one check is probably over $2, and an EFT order will probably cost society less than 10% of this sum when EFT is generally used.

EFT is a substitute for the use of bank checks. Therefore, the adoption of EFT will be most rapid and most widespread in those countries where the use of of bank checks has become most common, for instance in the U.S. and the U.K. And, in other countries, every shift from payment in cash to payment by check will increase the opportunities for, and the possible benefits from, the use of EFT.

The Federal Reserve Bank of Atlanta has published several valuable studies of recent and future replacement of checks by EFT. In the August, 1983, issue of their Economic Review, they reported that, in the U.S., the number of personal checks per year grew by 7% from 1970-74, by 5 to 6% a year from 1974 to 1979, but by only 2% a year from 1979 to 1984, presumably due partly to the growing use of EFT. They forecast no growth from 1985 to 1989, and a 25% decline from 1989 to 1994. They expected that the growth-rate pattern for all checks would be "the same" (p. 4). I suspect that, like most futurists, these forecasters have grossly overestimated the rate of future change.

In two 1986 issues of this Review, three authors reported that the 1985 volume of EFT transactions was still only about 600 million, a mere 1.5% of the volume of check payments, in spite of a recent annual growth rate of 35% to 40% (March, pp. 7, 20; April, pp. 23, 38). However, A.H. Lipps et al estimated the number of EFT payments in 1985 at 5.0 billion, about 12% of total check payments, and predicted that EFT payments would rise to 14.0 billion, about 17% of check volume, by 1990 (p. 218).

I offer no short-run predictions. I merely predict that over 90% of all noncash payments will be made by EFT before the year 2100. The chief basis of this prediction is that it is already generally agreed that the average cost of EFT payments will be far below that of check payments when EFT is generally used.

4. The High Costs of Payment by Check

Electronic fund transfer is, or will soon become, much cheaper than the use of checks because it saves the costs of writing checks, sending them through the mail, and processing them in bank accounting offices. Wire EFT also results in instant payment and instant verification of payment. EFT eliminates delay in payment, bank float, and bad checks. The marginal cost of using existing facilities for electronic fund transfers, like the marginal cost of using an existing telephone network, is usually zero. And existing phone or telegraph networks can often be used for electronic fund transfers. Finally, future improvement and growth in the use of electronic bank accounting machines, i.e., computers, will make processing of EFT orders ever faster and cheaper.

Estimates of the average cost of making a payment by check vary widely, as the next few pages show. However, I have not based my forecast of an increase in payment by EFT on any specific cost estimate.

(l) Separate Costs of Creditors, Debtors, and Banks

The future growth of direct EFT debiting and crediting of demand deposits will long continue to reduce payment costs. The eventual net total cost saving will be very great, probably over 80%, because the costs of payment by check are very high, far higher than is commonly believed.

Every payment by check creates substantial real costs to three parties--the person who requests payment, the person who writes a check to make a payment, and the banking system. For instance, on average, it probably costs the vendor over $1 to prepare a bill, insert it in an envelope, affix a stamp, and deliver it to the post office. The average costs to the debtor of opening the bill, verifying the amount, finding and writing a check, filling in the check stub, finding and addressing an envelope, finding and affixing a stamp, and delivering the envelope to the mailman are probably much higher because most noncommercial bill payers work much less efficiently than commercial vendors.

When the vendor receives the check, he must open the envelope, verify and record the amount paid, and take or mail the check to his bank for deposit. At the bank he may have to wait in line for some time before reaching the teller, and must then identify himself and wait while the teller adds up the checks deposited and records the deposit. If the vendor wishes to cash his checks, he must wait while the teller writes a very long number on the back of each check and counts out the cash. Often the teller must go to another place to obtain paper money of the desired denomination.

In 1986, over 10 billion bills were mailed to private homes by business firms. The postage cost to business and bill payers was probably over $5 billion.

In 1968, F.P. Thomson estimated that the total nonbank cost of using checks in England was about $1.65 a check. With an allowance for inflation, this implies a 1986 cost of well over $3.00 per check, to which must be added the cost to the banking system. He estimated the cost of one payment by giro at only $0.30.

The great majority of California banks will not cash checks for persons without an account in the bank.

Those that do charge betwen $1 and $5 per check, or between 1% and 1.5% of the check's value.

Workers who are paid by check and do not have a local demand deposit must go to specialized check-cashing firms, which usually charge at least a dollar for cashing pay checks. This suggests that the average check-processing cost to the banking system is over $1. The Wells Fargo Bank, one of the largest in California, charges $4.50 to cash a check for anyone who has no deposit in the branch visited, but most of this may be undue profit. Mayer estimated the total 1983 cost to the banks of handling 35 million checks at $15 billion, or about $.42 a check (1984, pp. 77, 87).

The Federal Reserve System made a functional cost analysis, with 1978 data, to determine the cost to banks of processing checks, and concluded that cost per item ranged from $0.35 to $0.50 per item. Since the U.S. price level has risen almost 90% since 1978, these 1978 cost data suggest that it now costs banks $0.62 to $0.90 to process checks.

Some banks are so eager to collect checks drawn on other banks that they use helicopters to rush checks to the nearest Federal Reserve Bank. And the Federal Reserve uses courier jets to rush checks between its branches. The growing use of EFT will soon end the need for such costly efforts to speed up check collection.

In October, 1986, the San Francisco city Department of Social Services estimated that the city could save $100,000 a year simply by eliminating the printing, mailing, and handling costs of checks mailed for the Aid to Dependent Children program and replacing checks with EFT (S.F.Chronicle, 10-23-86, p. 22). It also estimated that 15,000 recipients would save an equal sum they now pay to check-cashing firms. These figures imply that check-cashing costs averaged $5 per family per year (0.42 per check), and that check-writing and mailing costs also averaged $0.42 per check. These costs do not include losses due to loss and theft of checks and of money obtained by cashing checks. A similar reform in parts of New York City reduced the number of lost and stolen checks from 50,000 to 3, according to this news item.

According to M.G. Bender, Arthur D. Little, Inc., a research firm, estimated the total annual social cost of using 24 billion checks in 1975 at $8.2 billion ($0.30 a check). Since then, both the price level and the number of checks has risen more than 100%, which suggests that in 1986 check use cost over

$33 billion, and that the average social cost per check (including costs to non-business users) was over $0.60.

My own estimate of the current average <u>social</u> cost of check use is well over $2 per check, but I shall be conservative and use the $2 figure in subsequent calculations. Whether this estimate is accurate is of minor importance. The all-important fact is that when EFT is generally used, payment costs will be far below current or future check-payment costs, and this fact is generally accepted by students of EFT.

(2) Costs by Kind of Check

Estimates of the cost per check to the banking system vary widely because bank cost-accounting methods differ greatly, and because costs vary with the size of the bank, and the service rendered. Some checks must be cashed and others need only be credited to an account. Some checks go through only one bank because they are drawn on the bank where the payee deposits them. Other checks pass through two local banks, two regional banks, two New York banks, and the New York Clearing House. Thus we need cost estimates for four different check-handling services by banks:

1. The handling of "on us" checks presented for deposit
2. The processing of "on us" checks which are cashed
3. The handling of checks on other local banks presented for collection and deposit
4. The treatment of nonlocal checks presented for collection and deposit

As previously explained, an "on us" check, one drawn on the payee's bank, and cashed or deposited at that bank, passes through only one bank. However, it costs the bank much more to cash such a check than to merely credit it to the payee's account because cashing the check requires the service of a teller who must obtain, store, count, record, and pay out the cash involved, and also must identify the payee and the check. And it costs still more to cash, and then collect, a check drawn on another bank, especially a remote bank. Such service probably cost banks at least one dollar per check because this is the minimum fee charged by specialized nonbank firms for cashing checks on local banks. This fee can be as high as $10 for large checks. Banks can now afford to perform these services for some depositors free of charge, or for much lower fees, only because they benefit from creating deposits. The fact that they charge less does not imply that their costs are less.

The average cost to banks of handling "on us" checks, those deposited in the bank on which they are drawn (33% of all checks), is relatively small, probably less than $0.20. But other checks pass through 3 banks and a clearing house, and are physically transported from bank to bank. The average cost to the banks of handling these checks is probably well over $1.00.

About 60% of U.S. banks give immediate credit on deposited checks, but 40% do not. The use of electronic fund debits and credits to demand accounts assures almost immediate payment and/or receipt of funds. California banks now often hold out-of-state checks for up to 20 days before crediting the payee's demand-deposit account. Some same-city and in-state checks are held 5 to 10 days. And few banks inform most of their depositors of these practices, which differ widely from bank to bank. As a result, depositors often write checks on new deposits before they have been entered, and their checks bounce, for which banks charge high fees.

(3) Charges for Bad Checks

Most California banks now charge $8 to $13 for a bounced check, even when the bank quickly receives the specified payment (S.F.Chronicle, 10-31-86, p. 39). When customers sued the Wells Fargo and Crocker banks, the judge awarded damages that may amount to over $93 million. The plaintiffs had claimed that processing a bounced check costs the bank only $1. The banks claimed it costs much more, and the judge allowed the banks to continue charging $10 or more per bounced check, in addition to withholding payment for several days.

Actual losses to 11 major U.S. banks on bad checks exceed $1 billion a year. Total charges to their depositors for bounced checks were $3.5 billion in 1985, and the banks earned about $290 million in interest on the float created by withholding payment.

(4) Float Costs

One of the major defects of payment by check in the U.S. is that a period of time passes between the writing of a check and the actual debiting and crediting of the deposit accounts. Debtors strive to maximize the length of this period, and the sums paid but not received, i.e., the "float," because they can thereby save on interest costs or earn interest on the float. Business men and banks spend hundreds of millions of dollars each year on their efforts to benefit from increasing or decreasing this float. Business men deliberately create, and write checks on, deposit accounts in banks far distant from their creditors. They send checks to creditors by slow means of delivery, and they waste money on fast methods of cashing checks due them, at times even using special messengers and airplanes to present checks to the bank on which they are drawn. For instance, United Airlines long paid its employees in Illinois with checks drawn on California banks, and its employees in California with checks drawn on Chicago banks (Mayer, p. 31). And Merrill Lynch paid its East Coast customers with checks drawn on Tacoma banks, and West Coast customers with checks drawn on a Charlotte, N.C., bank.

In a recent study, A. Berger and D. Humphrey reported that the writer of a check gets an average subsidy of $0.15 per check due to his benefit from float. They also estimated the average social cost of check use at $0.68, and that of ACH EFT transactions at $0.33. The float subsidy offsets much of the difference in these costs, and sharply reduces the incentive to substitute EFT for check use (p. 5).

The full adoption of direct EFT will eliminate nearly all float, and will end the costly and socially undesirable methods used to benefit from increasing or decreasing the volume of float.

5. The Growing Use of Direct EFT

(1) ATMs

An automatic teller machine (ATM) is a machine which enables a depositor to withdraw cash from his bank account 24 hours a day, 365 days a year, by inserting a plastic debit card in the ATM. The withdrawal is immediately debited to the proper bank account by direct EFT.

The use of ATMs has grown much faster than any other use of EFT. The number of ATMs grew from less than 2,000 in 1970 to over 60,000 in 1985. There were about two billion ATM transactions in 1985, and about half of all U.S. cash withdrawals that year were done through ATMs.

ATM use has grown rapidly because ATMs can be used at any time of the day or night, any day of the year, and often enable users to avoid waiting in line in their bank. Bankers have rapidly increased the number of ATMs, because withdrawals by ATM cost banks much less than withdrawals through live tellers.

Unfortunately, most ATMs are owned and operated by individual banks as means of competition, and can be used only by depositors in the owning banks. Moreover, competition has resulted in a great over-supply of ATMs in some downtown areas, and an under-supply in other areas. Several writers have therefore proposed that all ATMs should be owned and operated by a single agency, a new public utility, which allows all depositors to use all ATMs. This would permit coordinated, socially-ideal location of ATMs, would reduce capital and operating costs, and would allow every depositor to use the nearest ATM. Such reasoning has already persuaded the State of Iowa to require that all ATMs be available to all depositors, and joint local or regional use is growing.

I predict that, by 2040 A.D., all ATMs will be owned and operated by a single agency, will be located so as to serve the largest number of persons at minimum cost, will be usable by depositors in all banks, and will be used to make over 90% of all cash withdrawals by noncommercial depositors. The resulting coordination and increase in volume per ATM will rapidly reduce ATM operating costs per withdrawal, as well as making the use of ATMs much more convenient for all depositors.

Some banks make no charge for ATM use because withdrawal of cash by ATM costs banks much less than withdrawal at a live teller's window. Other banks charge fees, typically $1. By 2040 A.D. all banks will stop allowing noncommercial cash withdrawals through tellers, and will charge a small fee for each ATM use, in order to increase the size of the average withdrawal. However, for reasons given in Chapter VI, the use of cash will decline by over 90% during the next century, so overall use of ATMs will fall sharply before 2100 A.D.

(2) Personal Income Payments by EFT

The second class of payments most suitable for early use of direct EFT includes all personal income payments—pensions, salaries, welfare benefits, etc. They are relatively suitable because income payment by EFT is already both cheaper and more convenient than payment by check or in cash.

In 1975 the U.S. Treasury Department began to make payments to individuals—bond interest, Social

Security benefits, civil service salaries, etc.—by EFT orders transmitted to some 15,000 payees' banks. This new method of payment not only saved the Treasury postage on about 180,000,000 checks in 1980, but also saved the banks over $50 million. According to Mayer (p. 122), it cost them 25 to 59 cents to handle deposited pay checks, and only 7 cents to handle an EFT deposit.

The U.S. government has actively encouraged its personal payees to accept payment by direct EFT. By 1982 about 25% of all such payees, including 33% of all social security beneficiaries, had accepted payment by EFT. IBM, Xerox, and other firms have also begun to make salary payments by EFT. I predict that by 2040 A.D. over 80% of all government and private income payments will be made by direct EFT.

The payment of social security benefits, pensions, wages, and salaries by direct EFT not only reduces postage and check handling costs for both payors and payees but assures more prompt and reliable delivery of the payment. Mail is always slower than EFT, and may be further delayed or destroyed by storms, train wrecks, fires, mistakes by postmen, or theft. Many thousands of social security and welfare checks have been stolen from post offices and mail boxes. An EFT order to a bank is far more certain to arrive on time, and it can arrive and be debited to the payee's account even when he is sick in bed, or on a long trip or vacation.

In order to induce more payees to request or agree to direct EFT payment, many payors will soon offer to share with payees some of the payor's savings from the use of direct EFT payments. For instance, social security beneficiaries may be offered $5 more a year for agreeing to accept payment by EFT.

(3) POS Payment for Retail Purchases

The third class of EFT payments for which relatively rapid continued growth is most likely is point-of-sale (POS) payment for retail purchases. Retail customers have become familiar with the use of credit cards in POS retail purchases, and the use of debit cards to debit their demand deposits is similar. Moreover, retailers will favor debit card use because debit-card use will cost them much less, eventually if not immediately, and will often guarantee retailers that the money has actually been credited to their demand accounts.

Continued growth in the use of direct POS EFT

will gradually reduce, and eventually end, the use of credit cards. By 2100 every retail customer will have a demand account, and will carry a debit card which enables him to pay for any purchase, or any cash withdrawal from an ATM, by means of a direct, verified debit to his demand deposit account. This will save the high costs of credit-card use (3% of sales volume), will often assure immediate payment to retailers, and will end losses due to misuse of credit cards.

Use of a debit card will benefit consumers because it will end the need to carry cash and/or several credit cards because one card will be universally valid, and because debit-card use will save the time and money required to write and mail checks to credit-card companies. It will benefit banks by saving them the costs of processing and returning checks.

In 1985 Lucky Stores, a giant California supermarket chain, began to advertise that it would accept payment by means of ATM debit cards, claiming that this would speed up check-out service. It takes much less time to offer a debit or credit card to a cashier than to write a check. And use of a debit card is faster than use of a credit card because the latter requires a signature by the user.

In 1985-86, Mobile, Exxon, Arco, and Diamond Shamrock installed EFT terminals in nearly 6,400 service stations in 23 states. Amoco plans to equip 4,000 stations in 1986-88. These terminals accept any ATM debit card, and many stations allow cash discounts on EFT sales since EFT payment is made instantly from the customer's bank account. The average for such a POS EFT transaction is 7 seconds (<u>S.F.Examiner</u>, 5-17-87, p. D18).

Credit-card companies now pay retailers about 3% less than the amount of each sale. To cover this cost, retailers charge cash customers prices higher than those paid by credit-card users. This kind of price discrimination is uneconomic. It raises prices to cash customers above the ideal level, and reduces their consumption below the ideal level.

The use of credit cards could be made far more convenient, and much less expensive, by creating a credit-card monopoly. This may occur. But debit cards will always be more efficient because they will be unusable when wire EFT is used and the payor does not have enough money in his demand account to cover the amount of the sale or withdrawal.

According to the Antietam Group's estimate, there will be between 10 and 20 billion POS EFT sales per year by 1992. The lower figure is larger than the number of bank credit-card uses in 1984.

Although most such past predictions have proven to be grossly over-optimistic, and although wire POS EFT payments may still cost merchants more than cash payments, rapid growth in the use of POS EFT payments is almost certain to occur as soon as retail stores have installed the necessary equipment. Once such equipment has been installed, both the average and marginal costs of POS EFT will decline rapidly as volume grows. The chief problem now is to persuade stores and banks to install such equipment before this inevitble decline in payment costs has occurred.

The use of debit cards to pay for retail purchases is already less costly to retailers than the use of cash or checks. There is more risk in allowing employees to handle cash than in allowing them to handle debit cards. And selling for cash requires retailers to handle amounts of cash which invite theft and robberies, and make necessary costly robbery-and-theft-prevention measures—safes, guards, alarm systems,etc. In 1981 there were about 23,000 gas-station robberies, costing dealers about $8.5 million. Moreover, when any retail customer in a line at a cashier's window or stand stops to write a check, or to have a credit card processed, he delays service to all those in line behind him, much to their annoyance. And almost half of all POS checks now bounce.

Finally, the U.S. government will eventually limit or prohibit the use of credit cards in order to divert savings from investment in consumers' goods to investment in capital goods, and thereby increase productive investment.

The growing use of ATMs, and debit cards, will gradually reduce, and eventually end, the use of travelers' checks by Americans inside the U.S. The use of debit cards will be more convenient than the use of travelers' checks because it will usually require no signature, and will enable travelers to pay bills for any odd amount, i.e., will not require cashiers to give change.

In 1986 less than 2% of noncredit retail sales were paid for by the use of debit cards. By 2040 this rate will rise to 50%, and by 2100 to over 90%.

(4) Payment of Monthly Household Bills

Many retail goods are sold on credit, are listed in monthly bills mailed to customers, and are now paid for by checks mailed to the creditor. Most families also receive other monthly or quarterly bills—public utility, medical, legal, tax, etc.—which they pay in this way. To eliminate postage costs, billing costs, check-use costs, and other costs, of this slow and wasteful method of payment, customers, banks, utilities, and other involved parties will increasingly agree to replace payment by check with payment by an EFT order to directly debit the customer's demand account.

In their Economic Review for August, 1983, the Federal Reserve Bank of Atlanta (FRBA) estimated that about 33% of all personal checks are used in POS payments for retail goods, and about 45% for home bill payment. They predicted that 65% of the POS checks will be replaced by EFT payment by 1993, and that 65% of such bill-payment checks will be replaced by EFT payment by 1997. Like nearly all earlier, and most later, forecasts, these predictions greatly overestimated the future EFT growth rate. But I am confident that over 65% of all such payments will be made by direct EFT well before the year 2100.

(5) Business Payments to Business

In 1982 the FRB at Atlanta estimated that 20% of all checks were used in business-to-business payments, and that, by 1997, 75% of these checks will be displaced by EFT payments (p. 37). In their April, 1986, Economic Review, they recognized that this had been a gross overestimate, and that less than 2% of all checks had been replaced by EFT payment. They explained this low rate by the fact that business firms often need to send explanatory material with their invoices, explanations too long or too expensive to be included in the then-used 94-character EFT message. Of course, other well-known obstacles to EFT use—loss of float, cost of electronic equipment, difficulty in persuading 15,000 banks and millions of business firms to cooperate, etc.—helped to slow the adoption of EFT.

Moreover, the amount for which the average business check is written is far larger than the average amount for personal checks. As a result, possible savings per dollar of payment from use of EFT are far less than for personal checks.

Nevertheless, several giant U.S. firms have recently replaced payment of suppliers by check with payment by EFT. General Motors has ceased mailing 40,000 checks a month, totaling $4 billion, to its 20,000 suppliers. GM Chairman, Roger Smith, is striving to achieve "paperless offices" free of clerks and filing cabinets. Possible savings to this one firm are expected to be hundreds of millions of dollars (U.S. News & W.R., 11-3-86, p. 54). Sears, Roebuck, which has an even larger number of suppliers, shifted from payment by check to payment by EFT in 1985.

In spite of these pioneer steps, less than 2% of all U.S. payments were made by EFT in 1986. Some European countries, however, have made much more progress. By 1984 more than half of all British payrolls, and a quarter of all consumer payments, were made by EFT. In Scandinavia and Japan the figures were almost equally high. The U.S. has lagged far behind Europe and Japan in adopting EFT primarily because it has far more banks, half of which are not equipped to receive electronic data.

The costs of nearly all electronic equipment and services have long declined rapidly while the price level has risen. There are very good reasons to believe that the cost of EFT will long continue to fall while other costs, including the costs of check use, continue to rise. Most of the factors responsible for the past decline in EFT costs will continue to act in the same way indefinitely. And every increase in the use of EFT will reduce costs per unit of service.

Even without any decline in EFT equipment costs, the costs per payment of using such equipment will decline steadily and indefinitely as the average size of banks continues to grow. The bigger the bank, the lower the cost, per payment, of existing equipment because such equipment is normally used at levels well below capacity.

6. The Obstacles to More Use of EFT

The chief reason why growth in use of EFT has been much slower than it should have been, and was expected by proponents to be, is that it is very difficult to secure cooperation and agreement among the 15,000 banks and millions of payors and payees who ought to use EFT. Many banks have never installed the electronic equipment needed to efficiently receive EFT messages, partly because such equipment has never been standardized and/or is still subject to frequent improvement. Many depositors have not even learned of the time-and money-saving EFT methods now available to them, and most others have never been told how beneficial such available methods already are.

The introduction of a new technology or system of organization usually requires that the pioneers incur R and D and other capital costs which eventually benefit all members of the industry. Most managers prefer to wait until they can benefit from the new methods without incurring the special one-time costs and risks incurred by pioneers. However, as soon as the use of EFT has been proven reliable and profitable by pioneers, a rush to adopt EFT will occur. This rush has already occurred in the use of ATMs.

Many U.S. commercial banks are too small to be able to afford the equipment required for low-cost EFT. Most such banks will cease to operate or be bought by large banks in the next 50 years.

One reason why charges for direct wire EFT are now high is the fact that both banks and communication companies compete for the small volume of business, which has created a very wasteful duplication of facilities and services. The communication industry is a natural monopoly. The larger the wire cable, the lower the cost per capacity unit. To build two parallel competing telephone cable lines between two cities is as uneconomic as to build two parallel competing railroads. Although the economies of scale in communications are very large, the U.S. government recently broke up an efficient long-distance phone monopoly and induced new competitors to build unneeded parallel wire cables between many U.S. cities. I forecast this mistke will be recognized, and that the U.S. wire cable industry will again become an efficient monopoly well before 2050 A.D., which will reduce the costs of wire EFT.

No government agency has yet assumed the functions of standardizing EFT equipment and methods and informing the public of the current, and probable future, benefits from the use of EFT. Such a government information program is badly needed, and will eventually be carried out, because few depositors trust the avertising claims of private banks.

7. Marginal-Cost Pricing and EFT

All estimates of the cost of EFT have been based on the current prices charged for wire use. Unfortunately, the typical price structure of cable and telephone firms is highly uneconomic because the prices are not based on marginal costs (costs at the margin). Electronic communication systems require heavy investments in fixed capital, especially in cable systems and automatic exchanges. As a result, they have high fixed costs and low variable costs. When they operate below capacity, as they usually do, cost at the margin is very low, far below the price now charged for off-peak service. The resulting demand is far below potential supply.

As explained in my book Marginal-Cost Price-Output Control (Columbia University Press, 1956), all prices should equal cost at the margin, i.e., variable cost, and the government should provide subsidies high enough to permit most firms to reduce off-peak prices to the ideal level, cost at the margin. Cable and telephone firms have never been able to do this because the government has never provided the necessary subsidies. However, since the adoption of such marginal-cost pricing would provide great economic benefits, it is only a matter of time until economists recognize this fact and approve the necessary subsidies. When they do, the governments of all advanced countries will adopt and enforce marginal-cost pricing, and the prices charged for most off-peak EFT will fall far below previous levels. Some EFT services may become free goods (see my book, Free Goods). This will radically reduce the cost of those batch EFT payments which can be made during off-peak hours without any significant loss of benefit to the consumer. Among such EFT payments are wage payments, dividend payments, rent payments, etc. The only EFT services which should be purchased during peak-use hours are those which require an immediate response, i.e., verification of actual payment, for instance, wire POS EFT payments.

It is impossible to predict when cable and telephone-system prices will become ideal, or near ideal, but this may occur in some advanced countries before the year 2100. In the meantime, these firms will probably sharply widen the differences between their peak-hour and off-peak-hour charges because this is often profitable and possible without government subsidies. For instance, such firms may establish, or sharply increase, fixed charges for peak-hour wire EFT, and use the additional revenue to lower off-peak-hour marginal charges. And sometimes a mere reduction in marginal off-peak charges may increase sales enough to yield a net profit.

Orthodox economists teach that prices determined in competitive markets are ideal, or as near ideal as we can achieve. This is an illusion, for many reasons. Perhaps the most important reason is that private firms with heavy fixed investments cannot afford to reduce off-peak prices to costs at the margin. This reason is rarely noted in orthodox texts on price determination or on the principles of economics.

Many economists hide or obscure the vital fact that most market prices are above marginal costs by defining marginal-cost so as to include a share of fixed costs. For them, off-peak costs may be as high as peak-hour costs because both include the same arbitrary share of fixed costs, and therefore become average costs.

The allocation of overhead costs to units of output is always entirely arbitrary. Many different methods of allocation are available, and there is no way to prove that one method is ideal. Therefore, the term average cost is literally senseless. It has no agreed referent. And when marginal cost is defined so that it includes some arbitrarily allocated fixed cost, the common practice, it too becomes equally meaningless. Only cost at the margin is meaningful and useful because it denotes an easily determinable and measurable referent.

8. The Costs of Fraud in EFT

It may seem that the adoption of a system of direct debiting of debts to debtors' demand deposits will permit many fraudulent debits to such accounts. But this risk will be negligible because all improper debits will be accompanied by improper credits, and both could easily be reversed when proven improper. Any deliberate or repeated practice of fraud will soon become obvious, and perpetrators will be penalized by suitable fines debited to their accounts. No firm will be able to stay in business and escape such penalties because every firm and every adult will continue to need a checking account.

To be more specific, one may charge that, if retailers are permitted to directly debit the demand deposits of their customers, some retailers will debit some deposits for purchases which the depositor did not make. There are at least two defenses against such unjustified debits.

First, if the customer uses a debit card to complete a purchase, he will be able to inspect and take possession of the goods he has bought before his deposit is debited. He will also be able to verify the amount of the debit before he allows the use of of his debit card. This should make it very difficult for retailers to use debit cards to debit depositors for fictitious or overstated sales.

Secondly, if any retailer made a practice of debiting customers' demand deposits for fictitious or overstated purchases, so many customers would complain to the police that the retailer's practice of fraud would soon become obvious and would justify both full compensation to defrauded customers and the imposition of a suitable fine on the retailer. The science of statistics is now so sophisticated that mere analysis of the number of complaints should enable experts to determine whether or not a retailer has practiced deliberate fraud. Moreover, repeated fraud would also result both in abnormal and excessive profits, which would constitute additional evidence of fraud, and in abnormal sales-inventory ratios, which competent auditors would notice and report to the police.

Finally, the general public will eventually be fully insured against such fraud by an insurance fund financed by a compulsory sales tax on retailers and service providers. Such an insurance system will give such firms a strong inducement to detect such fraud and penalize the offenders.

Fraud may injure business firms, as well as their customers. Fraud in the use of checks is now large because those who accept checks usually have no means of learning whether the check is good until several hours or days after they accept it. The full use of wire POS EFT will radically decrease such fraud because it will permit instant verification of any claim of payment.

The total cost to U.S. banks from fraudulent use of ATMs is now between $70 and $100 million a year. The reforms predicted later in this book (Ch. VII) will radically reduce such fraud because they will drastically reduce the use of cash, and therefore the use of ATMs, and will also make law enforcement far more efficient.

The rapid growth of credit-card use has resulted in substantial losses ($4 billion in the U.S. in 1986) because many such cards have been lost or stolen and because valuable goods purchased with lost or stolen cards can easily be sold for cash before the credit-card company has been informed that the card has been lost. Such losses cannot occur so easily when stores accept debit cards and use wire EFT because the store clerk is usually correctly informed that the card has not been lost and that the money is available in his customer's account.

In any case, current credit-card losses are not due to use of EFT. As Flannery has noted, "The excessive concern for security" in the EFT literature "is largely predicated on a false analogy between EMTS [EFT] transactions and today's credit cards" (p. 72).

9. Check and EFT Use Fees

Since each step in the adoption of EFT will reduce the large costs incurred by banks in processing checks, private commercial banks will soon initiate new, or increase the old, charges they impose for handling checks. The charge per check drawn on another bank will probably rise to $1 per check (in 1986 dollars) before 2040 A.D., and to $2 a check after banks have been deprived of the power to create bank money. However, the creation of PCA, explained in Ch. VI, will sharply reduce such fees.

These changes will speed up the rate at which EFT is adopted by the public. Fees will be fixed so as to cover only the costs to the banks. They will not cover the larger costs to nonbank creditors and debtors, but these costs will directly affect such persons and firms, and will provide additional incentives for minimizing the use of bank checks and increasing the use of EFT.

In 1982 about 25% of all checks drawn on U.S. banks were for $16 or less. If the social cost of check use is over $2, as I have argued, the writing of such checks is clearly uneconomic in the great majority of cases. Most such small payments should be in cash, or payment should be postponed until the next bill from the creditor is received. In fact, creditors should rarely submit bills for small amounts when they expect to submit another bill within 60 days. Higher charges for check use will help to induce debtors and creditors to delay payment of such small bills, and will reduce nonbank bill-collection costs for both debtors and creditors.

Although an EFT order costs banks much less than does the processing of a check, fees should be charged for all EFT orders in order to enable users to determine when it is economic to use EFT. Charging even a small fee will induce users to make less frequent use, and to transfer larger sums, on average, by each use. For instance, ATM users will withdraw larger sums, on average, each time they withdraw cash.

All such fees will eventually be based on real marginal costs, variable cost at the margin, not incremental costs, and will be higher during peak-hour use than during off-peak hours, when they may fall to zero. Such pricing will minimize congestion at ATMs, tellers' windows, and EFT payment machines.

10. Payment by Check, Computer or Phone

In order to use EFT to directly debit customers' demand deposits, retailers will have special point-of-sale (POS) machines, like ATMs, which can accept customers' debit cards and directly debit customers' demand deposits. Since such machines will be standardized, will use only one kind of debit card throughout the country, and will eventually require a wire connection with only one deposit-holding agency, the cost of these POS EFT machines will be far below the present level. Nevertheless, their cost will still be high enough to make their use in some very small stores and offices uneconomic. Such firms will probably continue to accept payment by check. The cost of clearing checks will be far below the present level if all are cleared by a single check-clearing agency.

Payment by check will also continue to be most convenient for those private individuals who receive some bills by mail. And many private persons will still want to transfer money to other private persons by check, for instance as gifts.

In some cities, credit and/or debit card holders can now order and pay for some goods by phone. They merely give their name and/or card number to the payee, who can then use EFT to complete the payment. For the customer, such payment is often cheaper and/or more convenient than to write and mail a check or to use EFT. The cost of the phone call may even be less than the postage charge for a letter, and the customer saves the time and effort required to write and mail a check.

However, payment by phone is not an alternative to payment by EFT. The phone is used to authorize the payee to collect money by EFT. And names and numbers transmitted by phone are far more likely to be misunderstood than those transmitted by mail or EFT.

Many writers have predicted that most homes will eventually be equipped with personal computers which will be used by residents to make direct EFT payments. The creation of a single demand-deposit holder (PCA), forecast in Ch. VI, will greatly facilitate such use of personal computers because they will need to be connected with only one such holder.

During the past ten years several large commercial banks (Chemical, Citibank, Security Pacific, etc.), several large security brokerage firms (Merrill

Lynch, Shearson Hammill), some retail chains (J.C. Penney, Sears, etc.), publishers (Knight Ridder, Times-Mirror, etc.) and others have spent many millions on R and D on payment of bills by use of home computers. And several different experimental systems are now being tested in one or more regious of the U.S.

Perhaps the most successful of these home computer systems is the Knight Ridder Viewtron home-information-and-transactin system, which began to operate in South Florida in 1983. Users of Viewtron can pull to their screen any one of seven million pages of news and data, can purchase a variety of goods and services, and can make payments without writing a check or mailing a letter. They can pay by EFT without leaving home. However, the needed equipment costs $600, and periodic service charges are about $30. Undoubtedly, such systems will be greatly improved and made much less costly. Moreover, they will provide other services than payment by EFT. But the need for such payment will be radically reduced as more and more debtors send their bills directly to banks. Hence, it is impossible to predict the future of EFT payment by home computers. In 1985 only 8 million payments were made by phone or by home computers (S.F.Chronicle, 5-18-87, p. 30).

CHAPTER IV. THE CASE FOR COMMERCIAL BANKING

My third major prediction as to the future of the U.S. monetary and banking system is that commercial banking, i.e., the creation and investment of bank money--bank notes and demand deposits—by banks, will be abolished before 2100 A.D. It will be replaced by the creation of government fiat money by a state agency which will use its power solely to stabilize a selected major price level. This, my sixth major prediction, will be explained in Chapter VIII.

Most American voters are completely ignorant of, or only very incompletely aware of, the nature of commercial banking and the chief arguments for and against it. Although these subjects are extremely important, they are rarely discussed in American periodicals or in radio and TV broadcasts. This was not always so.

1. Previous Discussion of the Social Utility of Commercial Banking

The rise in prices in England during the wars with Napoleon stimulated a heated controversy concerning its cause. Those who blamed it on the overissue of bank money were called bullionists. They included David Ricardo, Wm. Blake, Lord Lauderdale, James Mill, and Francis Horner. They persuaded the government to limit the issue of bank notes, but not the creation of demand deposits. As a result, English banks were able to continue to cause alternate inflation and deflation, booms and busts. The "banking school," those who opposed the bullionists and defended commercial banking, stated or restated nearly all the arguments for commercial banking, some of which are still used today.

During the years 1795-1830, when the first American commercial banks were being established, there was a long and heated controversy among Americans concerning the social benefits of commercial banking, a controversy reviewed in detail in my Ph.D. thesis, Theories Concerning the Social Utility of Commercial Banking (1932). Many eminent American statesmen—including Thomas Jefferson and John Adams—and many social scientists—including W.M. Gouge, Condy Raguet, Amasa Walker, J.A. Ferris, and Daniel Raymond—opposed the establishment of such banks because they feared the creation of an unsound and widely fluctuating note currency. At one time 9 states had laws prohibiting commercial banking (Miller, p. 21).

In 1794 John Taylor charged that the Bank of the U.S. had "a monopoly" of the local medium of exchange. He argued that all costs and profits of banks constitute a tax on the public (p. 216).

Thomas Jefferson asserted that "Private fortunes...are at the mercy of those...lenders [banks], and are prostrated by the floods of nominal money with which their avarice deluges us." He claimed that, in 20 years, the bank notes issued by the Bank of the U.S. had raised the price of a bushel of wheat from $2 to $10 (XIII, 277-78). In 1816 he noted that "Like a dropsical man calling out for water, water, our deluded citizens are clamoring for more banks, more banks...We are now taught to believe that legerdemain tricks upon paper can produce as solid wealth as hard labor in the earth. It is vain for common sense to urge that nothing can produce but nothing..." Jefferson was vindicated three years later by a banking panic in which many of the bank notes that had been thought as good as gold were suddenly worth nothing.

Although the chief arguments used by the proponents of commercial banking were essentially unsound, they won the day politically because the popular demand for more money was intense, and because it appeared that the proposed new banks would be very profitable. As a result, the number of new, bank-note-issuing banks grew steadily. The bank notes varied widely in value, and often became worthless when banks failed. The periodic overissue of notes caused repeated business booms, followed by bank panics and depressions.

The creation of a national banking system in 1864, and the Federal Reserve System in 1914, made commercial banks safer and more profitable, and reduced criticism of them, but all had to be closed in 1933, due to he Great Depression, which they had caused.

I predict that commercial banking, the creation

and loan of new bank money, will eventually be prohibited in all countries because the reasons for such prohibition are much more convincing than the reasons for preserving such banking. To make this clear, I shall first state and refute the arguments in favor of such banking, and then state and explain the arguments against it. The remainder of this chapter is devoted to the first task; the following chapter, to the second.

2. The Arguments for Commercial Banking

When the proponents of commercial banking first proposed the legalization and creation of commercial banks in the U.S., they used six main arguments: (1) that such banks will increase the quantity of money, (2) that they will increase the supply of loan funds, (3) that they will put idle money to work, (4) that they will increase the supply of physical capital, (5) that they will provide an elastic medium of exchange, and (6) that they will economize the use of gold and silver. These arguments were not new. They had all been used in England for over a century. Moreover, they continued in use in America until very recently. Therefore, they deserve special consideration here.

(1) The More-Money Argument

The original more-money argument for commercial banking asserted or implied that every nation always benefits from the creation of new money because this enables producers to sell their outputs more easily to consumers, who have more money to spend. In fact, the new money was supposed to facilitate all monetary transactions.

Since most individuals have always wanted to have more money to spend, and feel better off when they earn more money, they have found it easy to believe that nations also need ever more money, and always benefit from the creation of more money. Unfortunately, this analogy is unjustified and misleading. It is invalid for the same reason that the claim that what is good for General Motors is also good for the U.S. is invalid.

The more-money argument for commercial banking is the oldest argument for commercial banking, and has been used more often and widely than any other. Moreover, it is the foundation on which other arguments—the more-loan-fund argument and the more physical-capital-argument—are based, and it contradicts the "idle" capital argument for commercial banking. Therefore, I treat it more fully than any other argument.

In his Report on a National Bank (1790), Alexander Hamilton claimed that banks facilitate the payment of taxes and debts by "the increasing of the quantity of the circulating medium, and the quickening of circulation" (III, 394).

Thomas Jefferson noted and rejected the common claim that "the great and national advantage" of commercial banking "is to be the relief of the present scarcity of money" (XIII, 407).

John Adams, a political opponent of Jefferson, also noted and rejected the more-money argument for commercial banking in 1819 (p. 375). He was aware that both Adam Smith and Ricardo had rejected this argument because they believed that bank money merely drives gold and silver money abroad.

In spite of this growing acceptance of orthodox doctrine on this point, the use of the more-money plea for bank credit continued to be very common in the U.S. for many years. In 1826 Thomas Cooper, president of South Carolina College, although somewhat critical of the contemporary banking system, nevertheless accepted this plea as sound. He was convinced that the supply of gold and silver was inadequate for effecting all the payments of modern commerce and that banks perform a valuable social function by increasing the supply of the medium of exchange (pp. 37-38).

George Tucker, professor of moral philosophy and political economy at the University of Virginia, maintained that new countries are usually insufficiently supplied with the precious metals and that banks can perform a valuable service for them by increasing the supply of money. "By this facility of throwing an additional amount of money into circulation, whenever a more enlarged or more valuable traffic requires it," he explained, "they give a stimulus to productive industry, and prevent or lessen, the stagnation of business produced by that deficiency of circulation" (p. 181).

John Rae, who published his New Principles of Political Economy in Boston in 1834, also criticized Smith's doctrine that banks can not increase the supply of money. He thought that banks increase the supply of money materially and that this is their chief contribution to social well-being.

> "It may further be observed that the popular notion, that the advantages of banking are

limited to the substitution of paper for specie, and the creation to that amount of a fictitious capital is altogether erroneous... The real advantage...of the art, arises from its application of the floating loans of the society to the purposes of exchange;..." (p. 327).

Rae analyzed Smith's arguments in detail and concluded that, if commercial banking were abolished, the inflow of specie would not be sufficient to replace the bank credit destroyed.

"The effects produced by such an event would consist in a diminution of the number of exchanges, and consequently, of the division and subdivision of employment, and of the capacity given to materials; the transactions of many exchanges by barter, and the generalization of a large amount of them by transfers from hand to hand. Specie would only come in, in sufficient abundance to make up the balance" (Ibid., 326).

Even Condy Raguet, one of the leaders of the American anti-bank school, fell into this error of believing that commercial banks facilitate exchange by increasing the supply of money. After denying that banks create capital, he made the following concession concerning the utility of banks:

"How then, it may be asked, do the issues of paper credits by banks of circulation operate upon the communty, and produce that appearance of increasing wealth in places where they have been established?...These issues facilitate the transfer of the existing capital,...by creating an additional set of dealers with bank notes in their hands, and who are thereby enabled to purchase with the credit of the bank, what they could not purchase so conveniently with their own credit (p. 96).

Such an argument could, with equal logic, be used to justify an infinite increase in the supply of government paper money, for each new issue would create an additional set of dealers with money in their hands, who would be thereby enabled to purchase additional goods.

Henry C. Carey was peculiarly American in his views on the utility of bank credit, just as in his theories of rent and foreign trade. He upheld with unusual vigor the mercantilistic doctrine that nothing benefits a nation quite so much as an increase in the national store of gold and silver. In close accord with this theory, he held that banks confer important benefits upon society by increasing the supply of currency and its velocity of circulation (pp. 25-27).

While the popularity of this doctrine diminished rapidly towards the close of the period we are studying, a few writers continued to state it right down to the end of the period. In 1882, for instance, Robert Ellis Thompson, in describing the services of commercial banks, wrote:

> "To establish a bank of issue in a community where none has existed before, is to coin the mutual credit and confidence of the people into available money. It is to bring man into closer and more helpful association, by furnishing a new supply of the instrument of association and of the exchange of services" (pp. 154-55).

It is a notable paradox that many economic texts which note and emphasize the harmful inflationary effects caused by the creation and spending of new government paper money fail to explain that the creation and loan of new bank money has similar effects.

Harry E. Miller remarked upon this common practice as follows:

> "Even to this day (1937) it is probably not an unjust criticism of many textbooks on banking to say that they hail the economical _creation_ of media of payment as one of the great advantages of commercial banking and leave it to the student to wrestle with the apparent paradox that he is elsewhere insistently warned that multiplication of the media of payment signifies merely depreciation of the standard" (p. 103n).

To the present writer this paradox seems to be real as well as apparent.

The crude original more-money argument for commercial banking can be stated in more specific and plausible forms. For instance, one may claim that when a bank creates bank money and uses it to discount a merchant's bill of exchange or account receivable, it enables that merchant to receive payment earlier than he otherwise would, which in turn enables the merchant to re-invest these funds in labor and materials (Laughlin, 1931, V, 1718). It is easy to explain how any specific bank loan benefits the borrower. But the fact that individual loans benefit the borrower does not prove that the creation of new money normally benefits society. Most modern apologists for commercial banking have abandoned the crude form of the more-money argument, but still use the more specific beneficial-loan form of the more-money argument.

Although the pro-banking argument that every country always needs more money is unsound, every growing country needs some new money each year in order to permit an increase in real GNP without a decline in the price level for consumers' goods. This argument for bank creation of money has rarely been used, perhaps because banks usually create new money when prices are rising, and often call loans and destroy bank money when prices are falling.

In sum, the argument that commercial banks benefit society by increasing the quantity of money has two fatal defects. First, it ignores, and implicitly denies, the fact that the forces of demand and supply normally result in a general price level which makes the existing supply of money adequate. For instance, if the supply of money is reduced, the price level falls until the reduced supply of money becomes adequate.

The second fatal defect is that the more-money argument does not explain why commercial banks are needed to create more money. The need for more money can always be fully and cheaply satisfied by printing more government paper money. As explained later, bank creation of money has _necessarily_ caused large social costs—bank failures, monetary panics, alternate inflation and deflation, etc. Government creation of paper money does not _necessarily_ cause any of these evils. Moreover, when creation of government money causes inflation, the cause of such inflation is obvious to all. When banks create enough money to cause inflation, few voters are aware of the cause of such inflation, and sound measures to end it are far less likely to be adopted.

(2) More Loan Funds

The second chief traditional general argument for commercial banking is that such banks increase substantially the total amount of loan funds available to business borrowers. This not only enables business men to hire more workers and increase their output, but also lowers short-term interest rates and, therefore, the costs of production. Since banks must increase the total quantity of money in order to provide more loan funds, this argument is closely related to the more-money argument for commercial banking, and is subject to the same criticism. It fails to explain why the additional capital funds should be created by banks, for private gain, instead of being created by the government, for public benefit. Moreover, it assumes unjustifiably that whatever benefits the borrowers of bank money benefits society.

(3) More Physical Capital

A third possible argument for commercial banking asserts that such banks not only increase the quantity of money and the quantity of loan funds but also indirectly increase the quantity of physical capital. When commercial banks create new demand accounts and loan them to business men who use them to buy new capital goods, they help to increase the supply of physical capital. But, according to orthodox economists, all capital, physical or liquid, is the result of abstinence and saving. Who abstains from consumption and thereby creates the additional physical capital created by new bank loans? This question puzzled economists for centuries. Only since 1900 have some orthodox economists come to accept the following explanation.

When business men spend new, bank-created notes or demand deposits on new capital goods and on other productive factors, they raise the prices of such factors, or prevent declines in them, because they increase the demand for them. If surplus capacity had existed, some increase in the output of goods occurs, but this additional output is mostly consumers' goods, and usually comes after the new bank money has been spent, and therefore does not reduce the need for the abstinence required to create capital. This abstinence is performed by those who reduce their consumption because prices have risen. It is involuntary, and often unconscious. Thus every new bank loan used to purchase factors of production results in compulsory abstinence and saving by the general public.

When a government creates investible funds by means of taxation, the taxpayers are forced to abstain from consumption. When commercial banks create investible loan funds by creating and loaning new bank money, the resulting inflation forces the general public to abstain from some consumption.

Malthus stated this explanation of the effect of new bank loans as early as 1811, and J.S. Mill restated it in his Principles of Political Economy, but the great majority of orthodox economists and bankers long rejected or, much more often, ignored it (Beckwith, 1935, pp. 16, 20-23).

For instance, in his widely used Principles of Economics (1911), Harvard professor F.W. Taussig asserted that, when banks loan business men "great sums...created out of thin air...," they permit "the making of new plant, and the extension may far outstrip the real savings of the community." Later, he made his point even clearer by claiming that, when banks make new loans, "the command of capital is supplied without cost or sacrifice on the part of any saver" (p. 17). This theory is false because all investment requires previous abstinence or saving.

The argument that commercial banking enables borrowers to increase the national supply of physical capital is sound, but is rarely used by orthodox economists and bankers because they do not like to call attention to the fact that commercial banking causes relative inflation and forced saving. They fear that voters will ask them why the benefits of forced abstinence should go to banks and their borrowers rather than to the savers.

The fact that commercial banking causes large-scale general forced and unrewarded abstinence can obviously be used as an argument against commercial banking. Therefore, it will be discussed again in the following chapter.

(4) An Elastic Currency

A fourth and very common argument for commercial banking is that it provides an elastic currency, one that expands when the demand for loan funds rises, and contracts when it fails. Unfortunately, commercial banks have nearly always expanded bank money during periods of inflation, when their new loans increased inflation, and have often contracted their loans when prices were falling. The worst case of such contraction occurred during the years 1930-33, and was largely responsible for the Great Depression, the rise of Hitler, and World War II. In other words, the fact that commercial banks provide a perversely elastic currency is the basis for one of the most important arguments against the preservation of commercial banking, and will therefore be more fully discussed in the next chapter.

It has also been claimed that commercial banks benefit society by increasing and decreasing the supply of money during each year, in order to adjust to seasonal variations in the demand for money. But there is no good reason why each firm should not hold enough money to meet seasonal changes in its need for money. Since bank money and paper money are socially costless, there is no real social cost of maintaining idle cash reserves in periods of low need for cash. And the more-money argument for creating bank or paper money to meet peak needs for cash is unsound, for reasons already given.

(5) Displacement of Gold and Silver

A fifth argument for commercial banking is that such banks create costless money—notes and demand deposits—which displace billions of dollars of gold and silver coins. As Gresham's law explains, cheap bank money replaces dear gold and silver by driving it out of the country. In short, commercial banking economizes the use of gold and silver coins, thereby saving society the very high costs of using several hundred billion dollars of U.S. gold and silver coins. This theory goes back at least to Adam Smith. The fatal defect of the theory is that it failed to explain why the displacement of gold and silver coins by bank money is preferable to displacement by costless government paper money. And why should the benefits of such displacement go to private bankers instead of to the nation?

The displacement-of-gold-and-silver argument was plausible as long as gold and silver coins circulated, but such coins are no longer used in advanced countries. Hence, the argument is obsolete in such countries.

(6) The Use of Idle Money

A sixth argument for commercial banking is that it transforms idle money or capital into productive money or capital by loaning idle money to active business men. This naive theory is based upon the mistaken belief that money becomes idle when deposited in demand accounts. In fact, it continues to circulate from owner to owner because checks are frequently drawn on it. The actual turnover of demand deposits is about twice a day. When a bank is said to loan out idle funds, it really creates new money. The "idle" money continues to circulate. The "idle" money theory is based upon the old fallacy that banks do not create money. Yet it is often stated by economists who are well aware that commercial banks banks create new money when they make new loans. Those who use the "idle" money argument have rarely explained that this argument contradicts the older and more popular argument that banks benefit society by creating new money.

In his book, Wealth, Virtual Wealth and Debt (1926), Frederick Soddy, a Nobel laureate in chemistry, tellingly refuted the idle money argument for commercial banking, as follows:

> "Now if we concede to the banker the right to lend the deposits on the score that their existence shows the owners are not using them, we thereby double the money in the country and double the deposits. The existence of the doubled deposits is as clear evidence as before that their owners are not using them so they may be lent again, and now the deposits are increased four times. So we may go on and create an infinite quantity of money."

American banks have recently begun to pay interest on demand accounts, a practice illegal until 1980. This practice is uneconomic. It is based upon the naive traditional theory that demand deposits are idle or unused, and do not differ from savings deposits. In fact, savings deposits are the result of voluntary abstinence, which fully justifies the payment of interest, while most demand deposits are not a result of voluntary abstinence. The creation of all money causes forced abstinenace by the public, but holders of new demand deposits do not abstain from consumption, and therefore do not deserve a reward in the form of interest on their deposits.

(7) Payment by Check

One of the most plausible arguments for commercial banking is that it enables depositors to pay bills by check instead of with cash, but this defense of commercial banking has rarely if ever been used. The reason may be that this useful function could easily be performed by an agency which does not create money, and is therefore not a commmercial bank. For instance, a bank or other agency which held demand deposits backed 100% by cash could make possible payment by check, and could cover the costs by charging a fee per check.

3. The Defense of Commercial Banking in Recent Texts

Since the traditional arguments long used to justify commercial banking are so easily refuted, they are rarely stressed, and are often ignored, in contemporary texts on political economy or banking. For instance, in his widely used text, Economics (12 editions, 1948-86), Paul Samuelson did not repeat any of the traditional arguments. He explained that commercial banks "hold demand deposits and...honor checks drawn upon them," but did not claim that this is socially beneficial. In fact, these services are beneficial, but they could easily be performed by banks which keep 100% cash reserves of state money.

In his book Money (1975), after recording many of the bad results of early "wild-cat" banking, Galbraith called attention to the rapid economic development of the U.S. during these years, and implied that this rapid growth suggested that commercial banking had benefitted the nation. He failed to note that a similar argument could be used to justify the institution of slavery, which also existed in the U.S. during these years.

It is even more significant that he offered no other, more plausible, argument that commercial banking benefits the nation, and that he failed to discuss the arguments against such banking.

In my review of recent literature on the social utility of commercial banking I have been able to find only 2 texts on the principles of economics, and only 3 on money or money and banking, which offer one or more arguments in favor of commercial banking.

In their 1986 text, Economics U.S.A., E. Mansfield and N. Behravesh ignored all but one of the traditional apologies for commercial banking, the idle money plea, and stated two new ones. "First... none of the depositors had lost any money" and "The interest earned on the loan made it possible...to charge depositors less for storing their gold" (p. 169). Unfortunately, the claim that depositors have lost no money is false. Depositors have lost billions. The claim that the creation and loan of money reduces service charges to depositors is true, but depositors, like the general public, suffer from the inflation and forced abstinence due to the creation of new money. And, as previously implied, the interest earned on bank loans ought to go to those who are forced to save, not to the banks or the depositors. This book supports my conclusion that the treatment of the social utility of commercial banking has degenerated during the past 150 years.

In his book, Money and Banking, 5th ed., 1966, R.P. Kent (Notre Dame) stated four arguments for commercial banks: (1) they "pool the temporarily idle money" and loan it to borrowers, (2) they "monetize" the credit of borrowers, (3) they "provide a highly convenient kind of money," and (4) they serve as the custodians of...idle money" (pp. 112-13).

Reasons (1) and (4) are false because, as previously explained, the money placed in demand deposits is not idle. Reason (2) is irrelevant or incomplete because it does not explain how the "monetization" of private credit is socially desirable. It may be a vague version of the mercantilistic fallacy that any increase in the supply of money is beneficial. Reason (3) is more plausible but this function can easily be performed by other agencies, and will be performed, long after commercial banking has been abolished.

Kent failed to discuss, or even mention, any of the many reasons for believing that commercial banking is socially harmful, except possible inflation. His one-sided treatment of the social utility of such banking did not help students to reach a sound conclusion on this issue.

In his book, The Phenomenon of Money (1981), T. Crump claimed that commercial banks use "the temporary surplus [of money] of one sector to make good the temporary deficit of another" (P. 146). Apparently, Crump had not yet accepted the now-orthdox theory that such banks create and destroy the money they loan, or the fact that money in demand deposits is not idle or "surplus."

He also asserted that lack of bank money might force men back to barter. But any quantity of money can serve any number of transactions if either the money is properly subdivided or if prices have been adequately reduced. And governments can easily supply any needed amount of money. The "more money" apology for commercial banking is always unsound.

In his text, Money and Banking (1976), D.G. Luckett asserts that when a commercial banker claims that he "lends other peoples' money," one should listen because "It is not merely a cliché; it is almost a literal truth" (p. 143). In fact, it is a literal falsehood, and one which reveals the author's failure to understand the nature and function of commercial banking.

4. The Decline of Interest in the Social Utility of Commercial Banking

When writing my 1932 Ph.D. thesis on the social utility of commercial banking, I reviewed and criticized most of the English-language literature on this subject from 1650 to 1930. In preparing to write this essay, I have reviewed over 50 recent statements of the arguments for and against the creation of money by commercial banks. Therefore, I am able to express an informed opinion on the evolution of such theories.

I have found no improvement in the conventional treatment of the social utility of commercial banking. Some of the original naive and/or unsound arguments for commercial banking are still being used in university texts on the principles of economics and on money and banking, and the sound arguments against commercial banking are ignored more completely than ever before.

My most significant and surprising discovery is that the treatment of the social utility of commercial banking receives much less space and is much less comprehensive in recent texts than in the pre-1930 texts. One evidence of the growing neglect of this subject is that, so far as I am aware, no treatise, monograph, or journal review of doctrine on the social utility of commercial banking has been published since my 1932 thesis was written. The problems created by commercial banking have become much worse, but, apparently, no one has offered a new review of the literature on the social utility of commercial banking. At least, if such a review has appeared, it is not mentioned in any of the many recent textbook discussions of banking that I have reviewed.

Another evidence of the growth in the neglect of theories of the social utility of commercial banking is that many recent texts on economics and on money and banking ignore this subject completely. They make no effort to explain how such banking benefits and/or injures society. In my bibliography I have starred a large sample of such books.

How can this decline in interest in the social utility of commercial banking be explained? Perhaps the chief reason is that commercial banking is now an old, well-established, and very profitable industry. When it was new and strange, it aroused much more fear and criticism than it does today.

Moreover, commercial banks have become very powerful. In an era of struggle between socialist and capitalist countries, an age of periodic McCarthyism, American university professors may be reluctant to attract attention by criticising commercial banking. And the once conventional case for commercial banking is so naive and unsound that any serious, sophisticated analysis of it is almost certain to appear to be a deliberate attack on a pillar of capitalism.

The decline in interest in the social utility of commercial banking is also a result of the rising interest in the new Science of Business Administration. In a world where the Harvard Business School and its peers are dominant, who really cares whether commercial banking, advertising, for-profit medical care, etc., is socially desirable? If it makes a profit, social utility is irrelevant.

Finally, there has been so much recent change in commercial bank operations and so much revision of laws concerning such banking that the authors of texts on money and banking have had to devote much more space to these changes, and have therefore reduced the space devoted to the social utility of commercial banking.

CHAPTER V. THE CASE AGAINST COMMERCIAL BANKING

Having stated and, I hope, refuted the chief traditional arguments in favor of commercial banking, the creation and loan of new bank money, I turn now to state the case against the preservation of such banking, first briefly, and then more fully.

1. The Case in Brief

The most important arguments against commercial banking are: (1) the uneven rate of creation of money by commercial banks is the chief cause of harmful inflation and deflation, (2) commercial banking causes compulsory, unrewarded social abstinence for the benefit of banks and their borrowers, (3) such banking is a risky business which has resulted in large losses to depositors, (4) the creation of money is a natural and traditional function of government, (5) commercial banking reduces interest rates unduly, (6) it complicates and obscures the process of creating money and controlling the quantity of it, (7) it distorts payment charges, and (8) it concentrates too much power in banks.

2. The Case in Full

(1) Commercial Banking Causes Booms and Depressions

The first and most important reason why the creation of money by banks should and will be ended is that commercial banks have been largely responsible for most of the harmful inflation and deflation, and the resulting booms, financial panics, and business depressions of the last 200 years. And these catastrophes have caused enormous economic losses and vast human suffering due to loss of personal wealth and to mass unemployment.

For instance, the Great Depression (1929-40) was

almost entirely due to harmful creation and destruction of bank credit. This depression reduced the real national income of most advanced nations by 10 to 20% for ten years. It caused a very great amount of unemployment, which, in turn, was largely responsible for the rise of Hitler to power in Germany. As late as 1939, the U.S. had so many unemployed workers and idle factories that it was able to fight and win World War II with little if any cut in civilian consumption.

i. Commercial Banks and Borrowers Act Perversely

Business booms are caused by inflation. The more rapid the rate of inflation, the more intense is the boom. Whenever the price level rises, the profit margins of nearly all business men rise, and this induces most firms to increase their outputs. To do so, they must hire more workers, buy more materials and supplies, and, eventually, expand plant capacity by new investment. These actions cause the price level to continue rising, which again fattens profit margins, and induces more efforts to increase output. The boom continues as long as commercial bankers are able and willing to finance the expansion. Eventually, because of reserve requirements and/or central bank control, these banks are unable to finance further expansion. When they cease to do so, inventories build up, prices fall, and bankers become frightened and call some loans, which may reduce the total supply of money and intensify the fall in the price level and in profit margins. Sometimes, a mere reduction in the rate of growth of bank loans and bank money can end a boom and cause a business recession or depression. Small changes in the rate at which bank money is created can have immense effects on business profits, national real income, and employment. These social effects are ignored by the bank loan officers who approve or disapprove of individual loans.

In an ideal economy, the agency which creates money would increase the rate at which it creates new money whenever the price level begins to fall, and would reduce this rate whenever the price level begins to rise. In other words, it would use its control over the supply of money to stabilize some price level.

In our economy, nearly all money is created by commercial banks, but they use this power to satisfy the demands of business, or to stabilize interest rates, or to influence the balance of trade, and/or to stabilize the foreign exchange rates of the dollar. In so doing, they usually act in such a way as to cause inflation or deflation, or to increase the rate of inflation or deflation. From the standpoint of society as a whole, they act perversely. Their actions normally intensify inflation or deflation.

I have been explaining why and how commercial banks are able to increase the quantity of money unduly and thereby cause harmful inflation. It is equally true and important that they can fail to increase the quantity of money fast enough to prevent deflation. In fact, such banks, and/or their depositors can actually decrease the quantity of money, as they did in 1930-34, and thereby cause a serious deflation and depression. Since our commercial system is highly leveraged, depositors acting collectively can withdraw funds from commercial banks, thereby reducing the reserves behind depositors, and force the banks to reduce the total sum of demand deposits by amounts over five times as high as the total withdrawals by depositors. Since deflations can be much more harmful than inflations, depositors should not be allowed to compel banks to reduce the quantity of money. It follows that commercial banking is undesirable both because it permits bankers to increase the quantity of money too fast and because it permits bankers, and depositors acting independently, to reduce the quantity of money and cause deflation directly, and depression indirectly.

Moreover, depositors are most likely to panic and withdraw their demand deposits after the price level has begun to fall. Like bankers, they tend to cause or intensify deflation at precisely those moments when the social need for more money is greatest, and they tend to increase their deposits and help bankers cause inflation at precisely those moments when there is the least social need for the the creation of money. Both bankers and depositors tend to act perversely. This is an inherent defect of any commercial banking system.

To minimize these customary perverse effects of commercial-bank-loan policies on price levels and employment, the governments of most advanced countries have established central banks which have been given the function of indirectly controlling bank credit creation so as to achieve a more stable and/or ideal rate of creation of new bank money, i.e., demand deposits and bank notes. Unfortunately, central banks have also been given other, competing functions, most notably that of assuring that borrowers can obtain loans at low interest rates.

The Federal Reserve System, America's central bank, has the power to indirectly prevent or dampen inflation by raising the discount rate and/or by selling government securities, but it has repeatedly failed to do so because, like local bankers, it believes that the banking system should try to satisfy the demands of business borrowers, not the nation's need for stable price levels. The latest illustration of this malfeasance occurred in the 1970s.

During the years 1947-70, the stock of money in the U.S. (M1-B) rose by 88%, less than 3% a year, but in the next 11 years it rose by 6.7% a year, which caused the consumers' price level to rise by 90% (Newton, 14). When the FRS belatedly (1982) reduced the rate of bank money creation, it caused a serious business recession which resulted in a loss of real GNP or national output of some $350 billion in 1982 prices. Both the inflation and the resulting recession could have been prevented by proper control over the creation of money.

The richer the country, the greater is the possible decline in investment and consumer spending during a depression because rich people can reduce their consumption much more than poor people. Real income per person in the U.S. doubles every 50 years or less. Therefore, the next depression due to poor control over the quantity of bank money may be much worse than the Great Depression. This trend towards increasingly severe depressions can be checked and reversed only by sound government control over the quantity of money in circulation.

ii. The Banking Theory

As early as 1810, Erick Bollman, an American defender of commercial banking, recognized that both demand deposits and bank notes are forms of money, and that changes in the quantity of them affect prices like changes in the quantity of other forms of money. But he argued that banks can not overissue such money as long as they discount "good paper" only, i.e., as long as they merely satisfy the needs of credit-worthy business men (pp. 42, 59). This theory is often called the "real bills" theory. It is still accepted by many, perhaps most, U.S. bankers and business men, and by most Marxists.

In fact, business men are most eager to borrow new bank money when prices are rising due to a previous overissue of such money. When prices are rising, profits also are rising, which means that the notes offered to bankers are not only "good," but much safer than when prices are falling. Thus the fact that bankers can make safe loans on "good paper" usually means that such loans increase inflation and harm society.

The essential fallacy of the "real bills" theory is that it ignores the vital fact that when a million dollar bank loan increases output as much as it increases the quantity of money, the resulting percent increase in the quantity of money is usually 5 to 10 times as high as the percent of increase in the production of economic goods. This is true because GNP is normally 5 to 10 times as high as the supply of money. The issue of new state or bank money causes inflation whenever the percent of monetary expansion is greater than the percent of GNP growth. This vital monetary rule, which I once named the principle of differential ratios (1935, p. 19), is rarely if ever stated in texts on money and banking because it implies that nearly all commercial bank loans and investments cause inflation.

There is one additional reason why all additional bank loans are inflationary. The new bank money begins to circulate weeks or months before the new products financed by the bank come on to the market.

iii. The Effect of Government Deficits

Many defenders of commercial banking have claimed that the overexpansion of bank money is often caused by large government deficits, such as those incurred by the U.S. in the years 1970-80. But there is no law requiring banks to finance such deficits. They could be financed by voluntary foreign or domestic saving, which, unlike bank-compelled forced saving, yields an income to the saver. Government deficits rarely exceed voluntary saving in peacetime, and, in wartime, state-enforced saving is preferable to bank-enforced saving. The great inflation from 1970-80 was not largely caused by government deficits, but rather was largely caused by the harmful efforts of banks to satisfy the demands of business and/or to keep short-term interest rates low during a period of large government deficits. The banks should have reduced the creation of new bank money enough to offset the inflationary effects of government deficits.

iv. The Effect of the Oil Shock

It has often been suggested that the 1973-81

inflation was largely caused by the "oil shock" of 1973. But other countries suffered much more from this shock, because they were much more dependent on oil, and nevertheless, used monetary control to prevent the extreme degree of inflation which the U.S. suffered. For instance, Switzerland, which has very small fuel resources, suffered far less inflation (2% a year from 1974-81) than the U.S. (7%), (Newton, 13).

The same reasoning applies to other claims that foreign events--wars, famines, floods, etc.--justify bank-caused inflation. They may cause business men to demand additional, inflationary bank loans, but they cannot justify the granting of such loans by commercial banks.

For almost 200 years some anarchists and other reformers have claimed that, if banks made enough loans to workers who wish to establish a new business, or take over an old one, all workers could become capitalists and raise their real incomes, which would include some interest and profit as well as wages. The Kelso plan proposes that the government subsidize such a creation of worker-owned businesses by reducing taxes on such worker-owned firms. The great fallacy of these schemes is that they would require such an ever-growing increase in the supply of bank money that inflation would soon rise above 100% a year.

(2) Commercial Banking Causes Forced Abstinence

The second-most-important argument against commercial banking is that the creation and loan of new bank money by commercial banks causes forced and unrewarded abstinence. Since any increase in national saving and investment is socially beneficial, the fact of such forced saving may, as previously noted, also be used to support the claim that commercial banking is socially beneficial. However, commercial bankers have rarely used this argument, either because they are unaware of such abstinence or because they do not wish to make the public aware of it. The truth is that commercial banking benefits bankers and borrowers at the expense of the far more numerous general public, who would condemn such exploitation if they were aware of it.

As explained more fully in my 1935 monograph on the effect of commercial banking on the supply of physical capital, many orthdox economists have claimed that commercial bankers increase the supply of loan funds and/or the supply of physical capital without explaining how this is done. All saving, all loan funds, and all physical capital are the result of thrift or abstinence by some consumers, but very few texts on economics or money and banking explain who abstains from consumption, and why, in order to provide the loan funds invested in physical capital by the business men who obtain bank loans.

Adam Smith mistakenly asserted that, "It is not by augmenting the capital of the country, but by rendering a greater part of that capital active... that...banking can increase the industry of the country" (Wealth of Nations, p. 257). In fact, commercial banking has caused an enormous increase in both the supply of capital funds and the supply of physical capital in both the U.K. and the U.S.

i. History of the Theory

When a bank creates bank money and lends it to a business man, the latter normally uses the new money to hire workers, buy materials and supplies, purchase machinery, etc., and thereby raises the prices, directly or indirectly, of nearly all economic goods. The resulting inflation reduces the buying power of consumers. As an anonymous contributor to The Edinburgh Review, probably Malthus, explained in 1811: "The new [bank] notes go into the market...to purchase what is necessary... But, before the produce of the country has been increased, it is impossible for one person to have more of it, without diminishing the shares of some others. This diminution is effected by the rise of prices occasioned by the competition of the new notes..." (Beckwith, 1935, p. 8). This reasoning also applies to new demand deposits.

Dugald Stewart quoted this passage with approval, and Lord Lauderdale apparently also accepted it. So did Dugald Stewart (VIII, 449). But few later English and American economists did so. The great majority continued to deny that commercial bank loans cause an increase in the supply of physical capital. As late as 1911, Irving Fisher, the greatest American monetary theorist, asserted that, "It is...a cardinal error to regard [bank] credit as increasing capital by the amount of that credit" (Beckwith, 1935, p. 11).

In his influential Theory and History of Banking, (1891) Charles F. Dunbar wrote, "It is obvious that bankers created no new wealth by this lending and deposit holding" (5th ed., p. 6). The 5th edition of this classic (1929) was revised by O.M.W. Sprague, one of my Harvard Business School professors, who apparently still accepted this fallacy, even after it had again been refuted by several contemporary economists.

So far as I am aware, the first modern statement in English of the theory that commercial banks cause forced saving was made by B.M. Anderson in 1917. During the next 15 years the theory was restated, and often elaborated, by several economists—H.G. Moulton (1918), David Friday (1921), D.H. Robertson (1922), J.A. Hobson (1922), G.A. Kleene (1923), A.C. Pigou (1927), A.H. Hansen (1927), J.M. KEynes (1930, Cyril James (1930), S.H. Slichter (1931), and Beckwith (1935). In spite of the acceptance of the theory of forced saving by so many respected economists, nearly all later orthodox economists and banking theorists have continued to ignore the theory.

To refute the charge that commercial bankers are able to cause forced unrewarded saving, and thereby enrich themselves at the expense of the public, some defenders of commercial bankers have argued that the additional liquid capital created by new loans is voluntarily provided by those who accept the new bank money in payment for the goods they sell to those who borrow and invest the new money. This argument is unsound because all consumers, not only those few who accept the new bank money, are forced by the resulting inflation to abstain from consumption.

It is noteworthy that this explanation of the way the public supplies liquid capital to borrowers of new bank money has never been used to explain how consumers voluntarily provide borrowers of new government paper money with liquid capital.

ii. Current Neglect of the Theory

Even those sophisticated modern economists who are presumably well aware of the fact that new bank loans cause forced or compulsory saving by the public, for the benefit of commercial banks and their borrowers, rarely state this fact. For instance, it is not mentioned in the 25-page chapter, "The Banking System and Deposit Creation," in Paul Samuelson's widely used text, Economics (5th ed., 1961; 12th ed., 1986).

Although the great majority of pioneer advocates of commercial banking claimed that banks would create money in the form of bank notes, and although the great majority of the authors of recent texts on the principles of economics or on money and banking now admit that banks create money when they create and loan new demand deposits, some contemporary economists still deny this key fact. For instance, in his text, The Economy (1975), B.R. Schiller asserted that the primary function of [commercial] banks...is...to transfer purchasing power from savers to spenders" (p. 75). And, in his Money and Banking (1971), D. Fisher claimed that "banks only lend out money entrusted to them by their depositors" (p. 93). For another recent restatement of this naive fallacy see Economics USA (1986) by Mansfield and Behravesh (pp. 164-68)

It is difficult, if not impossible, to find a field of economic theory in which orthdox economists have clung to unsound doctrines so long and so tenaciously as orthodox banking theorists have done. For generations they denied that commercial banks create money when they create demand deposits and loan them to business men (Beckwith, 1935, pp. 26-33). When they were finally forced to concede that such loans do create money—out of air, so to speak—they repeatedly denied that the creation of bank money, like the creation of government paper money, has an inflationary effect. They refused to admit that the creation and loan of demand deposits reduces the buying power of the general public by raising prices, and thereby causes forced saving.

Finally, when more sophisticated economists proved beyond a reasonable doubt that the creation and loan of demand deposits cause forced, unrewarded abstinence by the public, and benefits only the banks and their customers, orthodox banking theorists simply ignored this vital fact in their new textbooks. To avoid any admission of their past errors, many of them omitted all discussion of the social utility of commercial banking in their texts on money and banking. And most authors of recent texts on the principles of economics have done the same in their chapters on commercial banking.

Although nearly all recent orthodox texts on money and banking have ignored the very important fact that commercial banks have caused forced abstinence and saving by the public, this fact is reported and vividly described in M.H. Rothbard's unorthodox book, The Mystery of Banking (1983), in which he forcefully argues that commercial banking harms society.

In his words, "As new money pours into the system...the early receivers...benefit at the expense of the late receivers—and still more, of those who never receive the new money at all...," Due to "a hidden tax...[inflation] the late receivers are fraudulently despoiled of their rightful resources

(p. 101).

In fact, nearly all "receivers," early and late, suffer because the "hidden tax" raises the cost of living for all of them, and does so permanently, not temporarily.

iii. The Vast Amount of Forced Saving

By December 11, 1986, the total amount of bank money in the U.S. had risen to about $720 billion--615 in checkable deposits, and 85 in bank notes. Nearly all of this had been invested, directly or indirectly, in the creation of additional business capital. The total value of all physical nonresidential U.S. business capital was then about $3,000 billion. Moreover, most of the $720 billion had been loaned and invested when the purchasing power of the dollar was two to ten times its 1986 level. Thus, it is likely that about 25% of all nonresidential U.S. physical business capital has been created by investing bank money and compelling the public to consume less.

In most recent years the increase in the value of physical nonresidential U.S. business capital due to bank-caused forced unrewarded abstinence has been greater than that due to voluntary, well-rewarded private saving. During the years 1981-86 the average annual growth in the net value of U.S. fixed nonresidential business capital was about $100 billion, of which some 60% was due to forced, unrewarded saving due to the creation and use of new bank money.

Incidentally, the rate of bank exploitation of involuntary abstinence is increasing. In the year 1986, both demand deposits in commercial banks and bank loans increased faster than ever in peacetime, by about $100 billion. This increased the U.S. inventory of physical capital by an equal amount.

It may be objected that new bank loans do not always cause inflation, and may merely prevent deflation. But the prevention of deflation has the same immediate effect on consumption as inflation. It forces consumers to do without the additional goods they could purchase if the price level had fallen.

Orthodox economists have often noted that the creation and use of government paper money is inflationary and forces the general public to reduce its consumption, but they have rarely explained that the creation and use of bank money has the same effect on consumption, and that, when new government money is invested, it has the same effect on the supply of physical capital as has the investment of new bank money.

It may be objected that some bank loans financed by newly created bank deposits are used to finance consumption, and that therefore my rough estimate of the effect on the creation of physical capital is too high. However, the use of commercial bank loans to finance consumption frees or displaces an almost equal sum of voluntary savings which would have been used to finance consumption, and can now be used to finance the creation of physical capital.

Incidentally, the use of a part of total bank loans to finance consumption does not reduce or excuse the amount of forced uncompensated abstinence due to bank-caused inflation because it does not reduce the inflation. In both cases, the amount of total forced abstinence or exploitation is roughly equal to the total amount of bank-created demand deposits.

(3) Commercial Banking is Risky

I turn now to a third argument, against commercial banking. It is inherently a risky or hazardous industry because it creates current liabilities, demand deposits, which are five to ten times as large as cash assets. Of course, commercial loans are usually short-term, and may be listed as current assets, but demand deposits are constantly due, and so are far more current than short-term loans.

Whenever a large number of depositors become alarmed about the safety of their demand deposits and start a run on a bank, the bank is in grave danger of failing. Reserve banks may help it temporarily, but many large banks have failed in spite of such aid. And a run on many banks may ruin the reserve banks, as it did in 1933.

It may be claimed that the U.S. commercial banks now have little to fear from bank runs because their deposits are guaranteed by the U.S. government. But this guarantee applies only to the first $100,000 of each deposit. Over $200 billion of U.S. demand deposits are uninsured, and therefore likely to be withdrawn whenever depositors fear bank failures. For instance, in 1983-86, when low oil prices depressed the U.S. oil industry, billions of dollars of uninsured deposits were moved from banks in Texas and Oklahoma to banks in other areas, especially to banks in New York City. Such movements can cause bank failures, perhaps, even the closing of all banks. From 1985-86, U.S. bank failures rose from 120 to about 150, the largest figure since 1933, when some 4,000 banks failed. In 1985 the entire state banking systems of two states, Ohio and Maryland, collapsed.

A recent study revealed that over 60% of the demand deposits in the 10 largest U.S. banks are held by foreigners, who can quickly break these banks by withdrawing their deposits. In 1985, Citibank held $53.7 billion of uninsured foreign deposits; Bank of America, $31.9 billion; Chase Manhattan, $35 billion; Morgan Guaranty $28.6 billion; Manufacturers Hanover $21.7 billion, etc. It follows that the next, perhaps the last, national bank panic, may not take the form of long lines of frantic local depositors clutching passbooks and desperately trying to withdraw funds, but is more likely to involve the quiet hum of computers processing the instant withdrawal of large uninsured foreign deposits by fearful money managers in Japan and Europe (J. Anderson, p. 83).

According to Howard Wachtel, author of The Money Mandarins, "Instantaneous electronic communication via satellite enables vast sums of money to be moved anywhere in the world in a matter of seconds.... Rumors—whether well founded or not—run through the financial trading rooms without the intervals of time needed to quiet them....In the cae of Continental Illinois National Bank in the spring of 1984, rumors about its inability to collect on defaulted loans ran through the international financial community like a prairie fire. In a matter of hours, billions of dollars were withdrawn from Continental Illinois, and the nation's eighth largest bank was near bankruptcy until a $7.5 billion rescue package from the federal government was assembled."

To minimize the risk of such an electronic panic, the U.S. will soon expand its guarantee of bank deposits to cover all demand accounts. Indeed, its treatment of the Continental Illinois Bank failure implies that such a guarantee already exists, although it has not yet been formally announced.

As long as demand deposits are not backed 100% by cash, it will be possible for some group of large foreign depositors in U.S. banks to force most or all U.S. commercial banks to close by merely trying to withdraw their deposits. Of course, the U.S. government could quickly print enough paper money to provide 100% backing for all demand deposits, but the temporary insolvency of U.S. banks would injure their domestic borrowers and greatly embarrass both the banks and the U.S. government. Why should not the banks and the government create 100% cash reserves before such a humiliating event occurs?

At the end of 1986, about 10% of all U.S. commercial banks were in trouble or on the brink of bankruptcy, according to U.S. deposit insurance officials.

To hide or obscure the fact that their assets are worth less than their liabilities, and that therefore they have no net worth to protect depositors, commercial banks have often listed their assets at purchase costs, not at current values. They are well aware that honest reports of the value of their assets would often frighten their depositors, who are free to withdraw their deposits at any time.

The U.S. banking system has repeatedly become insolvent, the last time in 1933, and the risk of such a crisis is greater today than at any time since 1933. In their September 16, 1985, issue, the editors of Business Week reported that "the U.S. financial system has become perilously fragile."

A quotation from one of America's best known economists, Robert L. Lekachman, suggests how great is the chance of a general bankruptcy of U.S. commercial banks. In an article in Dissent (Spring, 1986), he asserted that "An outright Mexican default [on its debt to U.S. banks] would set off a chain reaction of similar repudiations in Latin America and elsewhere. With the best will in the world, the Federal Reserve could not protect several leading American banks and simultaneously preserve investor and corporate confidence...the most casual of observers is aware that the bulk of Third World debt will never be repaid" (p. 135).

Within 12 days in February and March, 1987, three news stories suggesting the fragility of the U.S. banking system appeared. One reported that Brazil had suspended interest payment on $81 billion of debt to foreign banks. Another reported that the London market for "perps," perpetual floating rate notes, owned in considerable quantity by many major U.S. banks, had collapsed, with paper losses of some $2 billion. The third story reported that the Federal Savings and Loan Insurance Fund was technically bankrupt, and would need an additional $25 billion to cover past losses and prospective losses during the next five years. Since U.S. S and Ls now hold demand deposits against which checks can be written, they now function in part as commercial banks.

On May 19, 1987, Citibank announced that it had increased its reserves against loan losses by $3 billion. Other giant U.S. banks will probably soon follow its example.

The really great danger from bank failures, of course, is not the potential losses to bankers, but the possible effect upon the quantity of money in circulation. Nearly all U.S. money is created and validated by our commercial banks, whose failure may prevent the needed regular expansion of the quantity of money. Bank failures and losses during the years 1930-33 reduced the quantity of money in the U.S. by 25%, which was the chief cause of the Great Depression. This could easily happen again. The greatest evil of commercial banking is that it makes the rate of creation of new money largely dependent on the moods and/or business success of commercial bankers and their borrowers.

I have been explaining how fragile and insecure the U.S. commercial banking system is. It is noteworthy that the Eurodollar banking system, which has dollar demand deposits almost three times as large as the U.S. banking system, is more fragile and insecure. It has accepted over $1 trillion of demand deposits from OPEC countries and loaned an equal sum to oil-poor countries who used these funds largely to pay for oil imports rather than to invest them in productive assets. The borrowers continue to buy oil and pay interest only by borrowing more money. Thus, the Eurodollar banks, many of which are branches of U.S. banks, come closer to bankruptcy each year. And there is no international central bank to which these banks can appeal for relief when they need aid.

(4) The Creation of Money is a Natural Function of Government

Fourth, commercial banks should cease creating bank money because the creation of money is as natural a function of government as the power to impose taxes. Indeed, the power to create paper money or demand deposits is essentially the power to tax. Any desired sum of money can be raised either by taxation or by creating more money. Both methods raise the cost of living and compel the general public to reduce consumption. A 10% increase in the quantity of money has the same effect on consumption as a 10% increase in the total tax burden.

The theory that the creation of money is an essential function of government is so old and so widely held that most constitutions provide that only the central government can create money. Unfortunately, bankers and confused economists were able to persuade most U.S. voters and politicans that demand deposits are not money and/or are not created by banks. As a result, most of our money is now created by commercial banks, for private profit.

(5) Commercial Banking Distorts Interest Rates

The fifth reason why commercial banking harms society is that the creation and loan of vast amounts of bank money reduce interest rates below optimum levels. An optimum interest rate balances the demand for and the supply of voluntary savings. The creation and loan of bank money creates very large amounts of forced savings, which borrowers can obtain at interest rates below the optimum level because no interest needs to be paid to the savers. Of course, the interest-rate-fall due to forced saving reduces the volume of voluntary saving, and this partially offsets the effect of forced saving on interest rates. But both effects injure all voluntary savers.

(6) It Obscures the Creation of Money

Sixth, commercial banking harms society because it makes it much more difficult for voters and statesmen to learn how, why, when, and to what extent the quantity of money is increased or decreased. Most American voters are unaware that banks create money, or, if aware of this, find it difficult to learn how much new money has been created and why it was created. The monetary and banking system is so complex that even economists find it difficult and tedious to obtain and interpret the relevant data on the creation and use of new money, and often differ in their interpretation of such data. For the same reason, it is easy for monetary quacks to gain wide support for unsound monetary theories like social credit and other inflationary monetary schemes.

If all money were created by a single government agency assigned a clear and definite function, such as price stabilization, this agency could publish monetary statistics so simple that almost all literate voters could easily become familiar with the rate of new money creation and its effect on prices, employment, and economic growth. As a result, both voters and their representatives in Congress would become far better prepared to agree on national economic policies which prevent business booms and depressions and assure optimum growth in real national income. Complete centralization of the function of creating money is essential to effective and economical performance of this function. Division of such a function among two or more agencies is certain to prevent proper performance of the function.

(7) It Distorts Payment Charges

Commercial banks now perform two quite distinct functions: (1) the creation and investment of new money, and (2) the operation of a national payment system. They use some of the profit from the creation and loan of new money to subsidize the operation of the payment system. As a result, most prices charged for payment by check are far below the ideal economic level, and the resulting overuse of checks is large and wasteful. Depositors often use checks, which cost the banks over $2 to handle, to pay sums of less than $5, and even sums of less than $2. To avoid such waste, we must assign the functions of money creation and money payment to separate agencies. One way to do this is to abolish commercial banking, the private creation and loan of bank money.

(8) Commercial Banking Concentrates Power in Banks

The rise of commercial banking has concentrated far too much power in the hands of bankers. Since American commercial bankers control over $700 billion dollars of bank-created loan funds, and can determine which borrowers may use them, they have great economic and political power which they have often used to favor themselves, their relatives, their friends, and the politicians who work in their interest.

In the course of their normal business, making loans to business men, commercial bankers acquire a great deal of valuable inside information about future profits and losses, information which they often misuse. To be sure a proposed loan will be safe, they must ask loan applicants about recent and future profits. The answers give them information not available to the general public, and enable bankers to sell stock before losses are reported to the public, or to buy stock before higher profits are reported. They can also pass on such information to friends and relatives.

The Federal Reserve System and the member banks have often abused their power by increasing the creation and loan of bank money just before national elections. In 1968, 1972, 1976, 1980 and 1982, the FRS inflated the money supply and lowered interest rates just a month or so before the election, presumably to help the administration in power (Newton, 3).

The concentration of such vast power in the hands of a few men tends to make society less democratic, both socially and politically. Bankers have often used their power to discriminate against racial and religious minorities, and against women and political opponents. In other industries, concentration of power may be socially desirable, but not in commercial banking.

3. Socialism and Commercial Banking

For 300 years commercial banking has been a central feature of capitalism, and has greatly aided the victory of capitalism over feudalism. Commercial bankers have created immense sums of liquid capital and loaned them to capitalist entrepreneurs, who used them to buy up feudal estates, and to create and expand capitalist enterprises. It is therefore especially noteworthy that socialist economists contributed very little to the sound criticism of commercial banking before 1900.

Karl Marx condemned commercial bankers because they were powerful capitalists, but he never tried to refute the naive traditional arguments used to support the social utility of commercial banking. Surprisingly, he never explained how commercial banks are able to create immense sums of liquid capital without voluntary abstinence by any savers. He was apparently unaware that commercial banks compel all workers to abstain from consumption and thereby create vast sums of liquid capital, for which they receive no reward in the form of interest. His treatment of commercial banking was much less perceptive than that of John Adams and Thomas Jefferson. And this criticism applies equally to the early Fabian socialists.

As a result of their failure to grasp the main defects of traditional orthodox banking theory, the communists did not abolish commercial banking when they came to power in Russia and elsewhere. They confiscated all private banks, but they did not reject the arguments for commercial banking. Instead, they created a new and more powerful public commercial bank, the State Bank, which created vast sums of bank money and used it to make short-term loans to other state firms. Like capitalist bankers, they justified these customary commercial banking practices by referring to the social needs for more money and more capital funds. They even used the so-called "real bills" theory to justify commercial banking and to defend it against Jefferson's charge that commercial banks cause inflation. As Nicolas Spulber has reported (p. 176), Soviet State Bank credit "is to remain attached to" real bills, i.e., to movement of "real" goods. Here the State Bank operates on the basis of an old [banking-school] assumption, the fallaciousness of which is well known; namely, that money requirements and capital requirements are identical," [and that demand deposits are idle capital]...as Professor D.H. Robertson reminds us, the money created does not sit and wait 'tied around the neck of the goods but goes off on a round of visits of its own.'...Therefore, the policy of lending on 'real bills' in no way ensures that the quantity of money thus created matches the actual requirements of the economy..." (pp. 176-77).

As a natural result of the continued existence of commercial banking and the application of such unsound traditional loan policies, the Soviet Union experienced continuous and serious inflation during the years 1920-1945 (Spulber, 191).

4. Chief Conclusion--Commercial Banking is Uneconomic

The arguments in favor of the elimination of commercial banking are both more numerous and much stronger than those for the preservation of such banking. The most important argument against such banking is that it has caused, or at least permitted, very large and very harmful fluctuations in the volume of investment, production, and employment. The second decisive argument is that it has caused an enormous amount of forced, unrewarded abstinence, which has enriched bankers and their borrowers at the expense of the forced abstainers. Since men are very likely to eventually adopt any highly beneficial social reform, and since social evolution is now quite rapid, I confidently predict that commercial banking will be abolished in the USA, probably before the year 2050.

I also predict that, in the meantime, the proportion of economic texts which discuss the arguments for and against commercial banking, including forced saving and Fisher's 100% money plan, will increase several hundred percent.

For those who question this method of predicting the future, I cite the example of Condorcet, the most successful of all futurists, who in 1794 used this method to predict the eventual adoption of social insurance, political democracy, free public education, equal rights for women, and other major future social changes.

The power to create money is the power to tax. As long as private firms are allowed to create money in large quantities, they will use this great power to enrich themselves and their borrowers at the expense of the general public. They will also fail to control the creation of money in such a way as to stabilize the price level and national economic growth. Public awareness of these facts has long been growing, and will eventually force the U.S. government to prohibit all private creation of money, including that by commercial banks and the Federal Reserve System. The power to create money will then be assigned to a single government agency which will be instructed to use it to stabilize some national price level, probably that for consumers' goods. All other advanced countries will also eliminate commercial banking, for the same reasons.

(1) Two Methods of Ending Commercial Banking

The two effective methods of eliminating commercial banking which are most likely to be adopted are: (1) the adoption of a law which requires all banks to maintain 100% reserves of government paper money behind all demand deposits, and (2) the concentration of all demand deposits in a new nonbank agency which will keep 100% reserves behind all its demand deposits.

The first method would be the easiest to apply, because it would not threaten the continued existence of any existing bank, and is therefore likely to be the first to be adopted. The second method is certain to be eventually adopted because its use will yield very great benefits in addition to the elimination of any surviving commercial banking. This method will be discussed in detail in the next chapter.

i. 100% Reserves Behind Demand Deposits

Nearly all of the major arguments against commercial banking are over 100 years old, and were repeatedly stated and criticized in my 1932 Ph.D. thesis. The implicit conclusion of that thesis was that commercial banking has no social utility, and ought to be abolished, but I did not explicitly advocate such abolition because I suspected that it might delay or prevent approval of my thesis.

However, Irving Fisher was then reviewing the

case for and against commercial banking. He considered the same arguments I had reviewed, came to the same conclusion, and explicitly urged the permanent elimination of commercial banking by requiring all banks to maintain 100% reserves of government paper money behind all demand deposits. This method of ending commercial banking and all its socially harmful effects could be adopted at any time, and may be adopted long before the creation of a national check-handling monopoly.

In his lucid and persuasive book, <u>100% Money</u> (1935), Fisher described (pp. 10-19) seven major social benefits which he believed would result from the adoption of 100% money:

1. No more runs on commercial banks
2. Fewer bank failures
3. Reduction of the national debt
4. Making all of our circulating medium "actual money"
5. Eliminating the mystery of banking
6. An end to great inflation and deflation
7. The mitigation of booms and depressions

I too believe that all of these benefits except 4, which is trivial and/or badly stated, will be among the benefits of the adoption of 100% money.

The chief defect in Fisher's pioneer statement of the case for 100% money was his failure to explain how banks exploit the public by causing an enormous volume of unrewarded forced saving.

Fisher apparently won considerable support for 100% money. In his preface he listed the names of some 30 prominent bankers and professors who had already endorsed his reform. Among the professors of economics, he listed H.C. Simons, A. Director, F.H. Knight, G.F. Cox, L.W. Mintz, H. Schultz, P.H. Douglas, A.G. Hart, and others, all members of a group at the University of Chicago from whose "Memorandum" on the 100% plan he had "originally obtained many of the ideas embodied in" 100% money.

By pure coincidence, in 1934 I had written an article advocating the elimination of commercial banking and had sent it to the <u>Journal of Political Economy</u>, edited by the Department of Economics of the University of Chicago. The idea must have been in the air, due to the 1929-33 collapse of the commercial banking system.

In recent decades Milton Friedman has been the best-known advocate of 100% money. In his book, <u>A Program for Monetary Stability</u> (1960), he explained that:

"There is no technical problem of achieving a transition from our present system to 100% reserves easily, fairly speedily, and without any serious repercussions on financial or economic markets. Required reserves could be raised in a sequence of steps at dates specified in advance, culminating in a final rise to 100% in, say, two years. The Reserve System would provide the additional reserves needed to prevent the increases in required reserves from reducing the stock of money by purchasing government securities on the open market. Reserve money created in this way would take the form of increased Federal Reserve deposits meeting the increased reserve requirements."

Although Fisher's brilliant reform scheme attracted some support during the 1930s, it was ignored by the great majority of economists after World War II made the U.S. prosperous again. It is rarely mentioned in orthdox post-1945 texts on the principles of economics or on money and banking. Among the over 40 such texts listed in my bibliography, only five (Burstein, Smith, Timberlake, Culbertson, and Auerbach) mention 100% money.

Smith began his able two-page discussion of it by asserting that, "Although this proposal has usually been treated by its critics as unworkable, or destructive of private banking, it is nothing of the kind... But, it does not follow that it is the easiest or best way to accomplish the objectives" because the Federal Reserve might accomplish these objectives (pp. 237-8). Timberlake, a rare exception, devoted seven pages to 100% money.

Since Fisher is widely reputed to have been America's most able monetary theorist, and since the the need for 100% money is greater than ever before, it is hard to explain the gross neglect of his proposed reform. Perhaps it is dangerous to support such an idea after decades of cold war and McCarthyism. At least one able supporter, Dr.Lauchlin Currie of Harvard, was victimized by the McCarthy committee.

Recent inflationary trends make the need for adoption of a 100% reserve system stronger and more obvious than it has been since the Great Depression. The 1970-84 inflation and the 1981-82 recession were both due to failure to adopt a 100% reserve system. And inflation will soon again rise above 10% a year if this reform is not adopted. Moreover, as previously noted, the U.S. financial system is now more fragile than at any time since 1933.

The most useful function of banks is to collect and invest savings. To perform this function they do not need to create new bank money or to hold and transfer demand deposits, which are funds in use, not savings ready for investment.

When these three quite distinct and unrelated functions are separated and assigned to different agencies, each will be performed more efficiently becaue each agency will be designed and operated to perform one function only, with no conflict in interest between two or more functions.

If commercial banking is not abolished by the adoption of 100% reserve requirement, it will be ended by the creation of a national payment-clearing agency (PCA) which will hold all demand deposits and and clear all debits and credits to such deposits. The next chapter is devoted to the nature and work of this agency.

CHAPTER VI

CREATION OF A SINGLE PAYMENT-CLEARING AGENCY

1. My Third Major Prediction

The third major future American banking and monetary reform will be the creation of a single national agency to hold all demand deposits and clear all checks and EFT orders. It will be the sole U.S. payment-clearing agency (PCA). It will not be a commercial bank because it will make no loans and create no money. The functions of holding demand deposits and accepting and clearing checks (and check substitutes) on such deposits will be taken from all other financial institutions and will be entrusted to PCA, which will have no other functions than holding, debiting, and crediting the demand deposits of its millions of depositors, and reporting the results to depositors and the government. It will not accept savings deposits, create demand deposits, or perform any other function than holding demand deposits and transfering them from one account to another by simple accounting entries. This forecast is both the most important and most novel in this book.

To give PCA complete control over the accepting and clearing of checks, all banks will be deprived of the legal right to hold demand deposits and to accept checks and EFT orders against their time and savings deposits. Moreover, all other firms—security brokers, retailers, etc.—will be denied these rights, for the same reason.

(1) The Treatment of Commercial Bank Assets

The transfer of demand accounts, which are now bank liabilities, to a new agency (PCA) will of course require the transfer of an equal value of assets. But "equal value" does not mean the same assets previously created by the loan of demand deposits. The Congress will allow the banks to keep these assets (notes receivable and securities) and will require them to issue, and transfer to the U.S. Treasury, long-term, interest-bearing notes of equal value. This will leave the liquidation of old bank assets in the hands of the banks which made the loans. They should bear any loss due to their bad loans and investments.

The transfer of demand deposits to PCA will reduce bank liabilities by the total value of such deposits. If the banks were allowed to retain the assets which previously backed these liabilities, they would be suddenly enriched by an amount equal to the value of these assets, now (1987) about $700 billion. Such a vast enrichment of private firms and their stockholders would be uneconomic because it would not be due to any real contribution to the national income.

Although the PCA will assume all demand-deposit liabilities, it will not need any assets to back these liabilities because it will not be legally liable to repay any of its demand depositors, and there will be no economic need for such repayment. PCA deposits will continue to serve as money indefinitely, as fiat paper money does, regardless of the amount of assets behind them. If any such backing is considered desirable, the government will create enough fiat paper money to provide the desired amount of backing for the old deposits. As explained later, all new demand deposits will be backed 100% by new government fiat paper money.

The above analysis clearly implies that the immense assets backing demand deposits should be expropriated by the national government when commercial banks are freed of their demand-deposit liabilities. If such an expropriation occurred in the U.S. today, it could be used to reduce the national debt instantly by about one third.

How is it possible that such a vast expropriation of private property could occur without any reduction in the wealth of private firms or parties? The best way to explain such a vast costless expropriation is to compare it with the far smaller expropriation which takes place whenever the government prints and spends new fiat paper money. This process enriches the government because it raises the price level relatively and thereby forces the public to surrender some of its <u>real</u> income, i.e., to practice abstinence. It enriches the government without reducing the <u>nominal</u> income or wealth of private persons and firms. Indeed, the inflationary effect of the new money may increase such nominal income and wealth.

The immense assets now owned by commercial banks and used to back their demand-deposit liabilities were accumulated by the creation and loan of costless bank money. These assets are not identical with the physical capital created by the compulsory saving or abstinence due to the issue and loan of new bank money, but they are the result and measure of such forced saving.

Every new issue of fiat paper money or bank money increases the assets of the issuer without any reduction in the nominal income or wealth of other persons or firms. The commercial banks have been creating new bank money for centuries, and have therefore been able to acquire immense assets without any reduction in the nominal income or real wealth of other firms or persons. Therefore, it is now possible for national governments to expropriate such unearned wealth without any nominal of real cost to private firms and persons. The banks suffer no loss if they are freed of equal liabilities, and no one else suffers any loss when the government expropriates the bank assets created by the past creation and loan of bank money.

Another way to justify this vast shift of bank assets is to realize that if the government had not allowed the creation and loan of bank money, but instead had created and loaned to private firms an equal amount of fiat paper money, it would now possess assets equal to those now held by private banks as the result of the creation and loan or investment of bank money.

It is noteworthy that the eventual need for such a vast costless expropriation of commercial bank assets has probably never been mentioned in any orthodox text on money, banking, or finance. Even the socialists have failed to suggest and defend this idea.

(2) Anticipation of My PCA Plan

In a review of over 50 college-level textbooks on the principles of economics, on money, on money and banking, etc., I found only three which suggested the coming creation of a single agency which, like my PCA, will hold all demand deposits and process all debits and credits to such deposits.

In each of the five editions (1972-84) of their text, Money, L.S. Ritter and W.L. Silber included a seven-page epilogue on the future of money and banking, a discussion which was essentially the same in all editions. They forecast that checks "may well have vanished as quickly as they came," replaced by electronic fund transfer orders validated by a universally used "credit card," and transmitted to a "centralized and computerized" national payment center, "a National Ledger..." The mere "insertion of a plastic card into the appropriate receptacle will automatically credit and debit both accounts instantaneously." The authors predicted that "a National Ledger payment system will be possible in a surprisingly few years" (pp. 283-85).

Unfortunately, they also claimed that the adoption of this payment system will render "obsolete" the "hard-learned skills of Monetarists and...Keynesians" (p. 284). In my opinion, the monetary, banking, and fiscal problems with which these theorists deal will be as important and controversial after the adoption of the predicted new payment system as they were before. Later, I shall advocate a monetarist solution to the problem of stabilizing the price level.

Paradoxically, after predicting that Monetarism will soon become obsolete, the authors suggested that, after the new payment system has been adopted, a purely monetary method could be used to control "aggregate spending." The total quantity of demand deposits "will be subject to increase or decrease by any given percentage by Executive order.... If aggregate spending does not respond promptly in the direction and amount desired...further asset-valuation [demand deposit?] adjustments can be fine-tuned until the reaction on the part of the private sector conforms to what is deemed necessary..." (p. 286). I believe it would be better to use all new money to retire the national debt, but both methods are monetary.

I also reject their claim that all EFT orders will be "instantaneously" executed. Most EFT orders should be accumulated in batches, and transmitted in batches during off-peak hours to reduce transmission costs.

Finally, I reject their idea that the coming "National Ledger" should engage in "asset valuation adjustments." In my opinion the PCA should have no power to alter the quantity or value of its demand deposits, or the reserves behind them. Control over the quantity of demand deposits should be assigned to a separate agency, as explained in Chapter VIII.

Nevertheless, Ritter and Silber deserve special

credit for being among the first, perhaps the first, to adumbrate the idea of a single national payment-clearing agency in a university text on money and/or banking.

A second reference to possible use of a PCA-like payment system occurs in R.D. Auerbach's text, Money, Banking, and Financial Markets (2nd ed., 1985). He explained that, "As technology advances, the record-keeping functions [of money] can most easily be performed without...physical counting pieces.... The automated computer clearinghouse...[may] evolve. Everything would be done through computer terminals .... The country would have adopted a centralized electronic funds transfer system. Relative to this ...system, the U.S. now has a backward form of [payment].... Such a modern system is unlikely to be adopted" (pp. 12-13). The reason for this negative forecast is that "some individuals may desire to avoid records of illegal transactions..."

I doubt that all payments will ever be made through computer terminals. I predict that checks and physical money will always be used for some payments.

The third mention of a national payment-clearing house occurs in T.D. Simpson's book, Money, Banking, and Economics (3rd ed., 1987). He asserted that, "If everyone held a checking account with only one bank, the process of making payment...would be enormously simpler and less costly" (p. 28). But he did not advocate, predict, or even discuss this possible reform, presumably because he had little interest in such radical reforms.

2. Reasons Why PCA Will Be Created

The eventual creation of PCA is inevitable for 12 reasons: (1) it will radically speed up, and reduce the average cost of, clearing checks and EFT orders, (2) it will sharply cut the costs of noncash payments, (3) it will speed up and facilitate the detection of most crimes, and the conviction of most criminals, (4) it will speed up and aid the determination and collection of all taxes, (5) it will drastically reduce the total and average cost of direct collection of money due creditors, (6) it will aid, and cut the cost of, POS EFT, (7) it will provide government and business with many very useful new statistics, (8) it will transfer vast bank assets to the national government, (9) it will eliminate the waste of monopolistic competition for demand deposits, (10) it will sharply cut the costs of printing checks and writing EFT orders, (11) it will eliminate losses to demand depositors due to bank failures, and (12) it will greatly reduce losses due to bad checks and EFT orders.

(1) Creation of PCA Will Cut Clearing Costs

The creation of PCA will radically reduce payment-clearing costs, probably by over 80%, in several ways.

It will reduce the number of payment-clearing offices from many thousands to one. At present, some 20,000 banks and other firms hold demand deposits and clear all "on us" checks and check substitutes. Most of these offices handle such a small number of checks that they cannot achieve anywhere near the full potential economies of scale. Most checks which are not "on us" now pass through two or three banks and one of 32 regional automatic clearing houses (ACHs), which, on average, operate at about 10% of capacity.

According to a 1981 report by the Mellon Bank, "the average check is handled by 2.4 banks." Add the payor and payee, and the total is 4.4 handlings per check. But that is only the start. Within the 2.4 banks each check is handled 15 to 25 times for sorting, entry, and collection. In addition, on average, the post office handles each mailed check 3 to 5 times in its collection, sorting, forwarding, and delivery of mail. By 1990, it may take 2.0 trillion handlings to keep the check payment system functioning. When Martin Mayer traced a check he had written near New York City, he found that his check passed through eight separate offices, and was handled by nearly 24 people, before it was returned to him (p. 77).

Reducing the number of offices in which demand deposits are debited and credited from thousands to one should yield very large economies of scale, without any improvement in the machines and methods used to clear checks.

The chief defect of the existing batch-processing EFT system is that it uses 32 regional clearing houses, all of which required investment in expensive physical equipment. According to B.K. Stone, of the Georgia Institute of Technology, "the fixed cost for 32 processing plants is probably more than 20 times greater than the fixed cost of a single, central location" (p. 29).

The concentration of all payment-processing in a single building will yield all the numerous economies normally made possible by a very large increase in the scale of construction. But this is not the chief reform needed to achieve the maximum economies of scale. The chief reform needed is the concentration of all demand deposits in a single national office. This will further radically reduce the cost of holding such deposits and debiting and crediting all payments to them. Under the present system, such debits and credits must be classified by payee bank and transmitted to over 20,000 agencies which now hold demand accounts and make debits and credits to them. It is noteworthy that Stone clearly understood the possible economies from merging all clearing houses, but failed to mention the far greater possible economies from merging all processing of debits and credits to demand accounts.

Moreover, a single national clearing house for all payments (PCA) will be able to design and use far larger and more efficient computers and/or accounting machines than any previously in use. It will also be able to practice a much greater and more efficient division of labor among both workers and machines.

In addition to radically reducing payment costs, the creation of PCA will greatly increase the speed of payment. All EFT orders will be sent directly to PCA. None will be sent to correspondent banks or to regional clearing houses, which take time to process them. And those who prepare and transmit EFT orders will be able to do so far more rapidly because all orders will be sent to the same address.

(2) Use of PCA Will Cut Payment Costs

The creation and use of PCA will radically reduce the costs of making wage payments, insurance benefit payments, dividend payments, interest payments, etc., because the payor will be able to send all his payment orders to a single national agency, PCA, instead of sending them to many different demand-deposit-holding agencies. This great cost reduction will be achieved in the accounting offices of payors, and is additional to any saving in the costs to banks and clearing houses of clearing checks and EFT orders.

The U.S. Social Security Administration (SSA) now sends social security benefits directly to the banks of several million beneficiaries who have approved this most efficient method of benefit payment. Since these beneficiaries have demand accounts in some 20,000 banks, the SSA must determine the name of the bank used by each beneficiary, classify benefits by bank, and send EFT payment orders directly to 20,000 different banks, or to the 32 regional clearing houses, which now classify the EFT orders and forward batches of orders to other regional clearing houses, which eventually send them to 20,000 banks. How much cheaper, faster, and more error-free it would be if the SSA could send all EFT payment orders, unclassified, to a single clearing house, PCA.

A large firm like Ford Motors may have tens of thousands of suppliers, who must be paid each month. The most economical method of payment is to directly credit their demand accounts by EFT. This may now require sending a separate, unique EFT order, directly or indirectly, to each of some 20,000 banks. If all suppliers, and other creditors had their demand deposits in a single place (PCA), Ford could make all payments each month by means of a single electronic message to PCA. And this message need not list any payee and his credit unless the amount due has changed since the last message was sent. Ford could instruct the PCA to repeat th same dividend, interest, salary, and other payments until it receives orders to change such payments.

The creation of PCA will also yield similar but much smaller payment savings to all nonbusiness depositors, who now mail an average of 20 checks a month to 20 different addresses. Most bills will be sent directly to the PCA, so the need to write checks will be radically reduced for all holders of personal demand deposits. Of course, this saving to domestic depositors will be due to the use of direct billing by debtors, not to the creation of PCA. But some bills will still go to private homes.

(3) PCA Will Facilitate Detection of Crime

The creation of PCA will greatly facilitate the use of bank records to detect and penalize any monetary crime because it will collect in one place all the bank records useful to police. Instead of visiting, writing, or calling many different banks in order to obtain relevant evidence of monetary crime, police will need to contact only the PCA.

Moreover, the PCA will accept only one account from each person, and will reject deposits from persons using false names. Its statements to personal depositors will include all the income and payments of each depositor. At present, any criminal can maintain checking accounts in several different banks under his own name, or under different names, and can hide or obscure the nature of his income and payments by frequently shifting funds from one bank account to another.

(4) PCA Will Facilitate Tax Collection

The creation and use of PCA will speed up and aid the collection of all taxes for the same reasons that it will speed up and improve the detection of monetary crime.

These last two reasons why the creation of PCA is inevitable (3 and 4) are so significant that they will be elaborated in a separate, immediately following chapter.

(5) Use of PCA Will Cut Direct Billing Costs

The use of PCA will drastically reduce the costs previously incurred by debtors in sending bills and invoices to the commercial banks of their creditors because debtors will be able to mail all bills to a single agency, PCA, instead of mailing them, directly or indirectly, to up to 20,000 banks.

This saving is additional to any saving from the adoption of direct billing or EFT, and to any saving in the cost of clearing checks in clearing houses. Direct billing saves large sums even when bills must be sent to many banks. The creation of PCA will yield large additional savings.

(6) Use of PCA Will Cut Costs of POS EFT

In the absence of PCA, when retail stores begin to use wire EFT at points of sale to obtain immediate guaranteed payment from debit-card-using customers, they will have to have direct wire connections with each bank which participates in such payment to retail stores. Such multiple wire use would be unduly costly. The creation of PCA will permit each retail store to accept POS EFT payment from over 100,000,000 customers by means of a single wire connection to PCA. As a result, direct POS EFT payment will become far less expensive than it now is. This new saving is an additional saving.

If POS EFT payment requires the use of regional clearing houses, retailers cannot get immediate confirmation of payment. Moreover, the average payment must be handled by two to four banks and clearing houses.

(7) PCA Will Provide Valuable New Statistics

When the processing of all demand-deposit debits and credits has been concentrated in a single agency, that agency (PCA) will become able to prepare new statistical data of great value both to business men and to government officials. For instance, it will become able to supply business men with: (1) daily reports on their total noncash monetary receipts and/or expenditures, broken down by plant, office, or other reporting agency, (2) daily reports on noncash sales, usually over 95% of all sales, similarly broken down, (3) weekly reports on wage payments, fuel costs, raw material purchases, etc., if these expenses have been separately reported, which would be easy to do,and (4) similar reports for any industry as a whole, or for the nation.

PCA will also probably be able to supply the U.S. government with data it has never before been able to secure, including: (1) weekly reports on total retail sales, by state or city, (2) weekly reports on total wages paid, broken down by firm and/or industry, (3) daily reports on total debits to demand accounts, broken down by firm or industry, (4) weekly reports on total tax payments, similarly broken down, (5) weekly reports on total social security payments, (6) weekly reports on total wage and salary payments by federal, state, and/or local government agencies, broken down by category if reporting offices supply such detail. And a great many other classes of total national monetary receipts and expenditures could be provided if reporting agencies agree to supply the basic data, or are required by law to do so. The additional costs would be small.

These additional statistics will be of very great value, both to government agencies and to all social scientists. All social science is based on statistics.

It must be emphasized that the claimed increase in the amount of useful statistics will result from the concentration of all payment data in a single national office, not from the use of EFT, as Flannery and Jaffe once claimed (p. 193).

(8) Vast Shift of Bank Assets to Government

As explained earlier, the transfer of all demand-deposit liabilities from commercial banks to the PCA will require the transfer of an equal value of bank assets from the banks to the national government. These assets are now worth some $700 billion, and their value will continue to rise rapidly until PCA is established. Therefore, the creation of PCA will result in an immense one-time shift of wealth to the government, a shift which will enrich the state without any reduction in the net wealth of any private firm or person. Nearly all of this increase in government assets will be used to reduce the national debt, and this drastic reduction will yield many economic benefits.

(9) Monopoly Will End Costs of Competition

It is noteworthy that the final stage in the integration of any industry, the creation of a monopoly, yields not only additional economies of scale and scope, but also yields other economies of monopoly, including a marked reduction in both selling and producing costs. Since it has no competition, a monopoly can eliminate nearly all costs of aggressive selling—advertising, personal sales effort, search for customers, high rents due to choice location, duplication of facilities, etc. It can also markedly reduce production costs by simplifying and standardizing its products. Monopolistic competition has led to the production of an excessive variety of goods and/or services in most industries. Only a monopoly can achieve an optimum degree of reduction in the variety of its products.

For instance, in the banking industry only the creation of a monopoly can achieve complete standardization of check and deposit forms, of ATMs, of EFT equipment, of all office equipment, etc. Only a monopoly can locate its ATMs so as to minimize uneconomic duplication of facilities (2, 3, or 4 ATMs in one city block) and provide optimum access to ATMs. Only a monopoly can concentrate all demand deposits and check clearing in a single regional or national office so as to make all regional or national checks "on us," and thus minimize clearance costs. Only a monopoly can spend an ideal amount on specialized employee training because it has no competitors to hire away its specially trained employees, or can spend on R and D, confident that no competitor can use the results of such R and D.

The business of handling bank checks and check substitutes (EFT) is a natural monopoly for the same reason that the local postal or telephone system is a natural monopoly. All checks should pass through a single check-clearing office for the same reason that all local mail or phone calls should pass through the same local post office or telephone exchange. Competition is as wasteful and uneconomic in one industry as in the other. There are plausible arguments for competition in the collection and investment of savings, but there are none for competition in the handling of bank checks and EFT orders.

The commercial banking industry operates under

conditions of monopolistic competition. Banks in one-bank towns are virtual monopolies, and those in cities with two or more banks are duopolies or oligopolies. They minimize price competition and maximize competition in service and advertising. One result of this is that they have invested huge sums in handsome, imposing, and expensive bank buildings in high-rent urban areas. The creation of PCA will render surplus over half of these buildings, probably worth over $15 billion. The net effect will be the equivalent of an addition to the national wealth of over $10 billion, and a significant reduction in street congestion in high-rent areas.

(10) It Will Cut Costs of Checks and EFT Orders

The creation and universal use of PCA will reduce the amount of information needed on each check and in each EFT order. It will no longer be necessary to show the name and address of one of some 20,000 banks on a check, or to include them in EFT orders, because all checks and orders will go to the PCA, where they will be "on us." This reduction in content will reduce the cost of printing checks, and will also permit the complete standardization of checks throughout the nation, which will reduce the cost of printing, distributing, and storing blank checks. The same reduction in content will reduce the length of every EFT order, and thereby cut the cost of preparing, transmitting, reading, and responding to all EFT orders.

(11) No Losses to Depositors

Every year some commercial banks fail, and their depositors suffer large losses. Many deposits are insured, but payment of insurance benefits takes time, often many weeks. And depositors whose deposits are not insured may receive no payment. The creation and universal use of PCA will end all such losses because PCA will make no bad loans. Moreover, all its demand depositors will be backed 100% by government paper money.

It may seem that this benefit could be obtained, without creation of PCA, by requiring all commercial banks to maintain 100% cash reserves behind all demand deposits, but, with 20,000 demand-deposit-holding banks, some are likely to disobey such a law when nearing bankruptcy. It would be much easier to enforce a 100% reserve rule on one agency, PCA, than on many competing commercial banks.

Most commercial banks perform several functions in addition to commercial banking. For instance, they trade in gold, silver, and foreign exchange, and may incur large losses in these operations, losses which fall partly on demand depositors when a commercial bank fails. PCA will not perform such functions and will have no such losses to pass on to its depositors.

(12) Reduction of Bad Check Losses

Both the creation of PCA and the use of direct wire EFT will help to radically reduce losses from bad checks and fraud. It now usually takes several days for banks to learn that bad checks are bad, and to report this fact to the payee. During this time the check writer may move to a different city, state, or country, without leaving a new address. So many bad checks are written, and it is so hard to trace bad-check writers, that police usually make little if any effort to find and arrest nonresident bad-check writers. Moreover, when they are arrested, court proceedings are costly, and payees rarely recover their losses.

With PCA in operation, victims of bad-check writers will learn of their loss far more quickly, and will have a far greater chance of recovering their loss. The cost of recovery will be negligible, because normally it will only require reversal of a bookkeeping entry in two deposit accounts. No bad-check writer will be able to evade such repayment because each will be required to receive all income through PCA, which will always have his current address.

Any bad check losses not thus recovered will be borne by PCA and added to the cost covered by its use fees. In other words, all such losses will be covered by insurance.

Since there are now many different kinds of both credit cards and debit cards in use in the U.S., it is relatively difficult for retail clerks and cashiers to become familiar with them and able to detect counterfeit cards and misuse of legitimate cards. One of the major benefits of the creation of a payment-clearing monopoly is that this will result in universal use of a single sophisticated debit card familiar to all sales clerks and cashiers. This will sharply reduce losses due to misuse of credit and debit cards.

Another advantage of universal use and acceptance of a single debit card is that card holders will never have to look for a place where their card is accepted. They will know that all large, and many small, firms accept it.

The use of PCA records to detect crimes and prosecute criminals will be discussed in detail in Chapter VII.

(13) Estimate of Total Savings

In Chapter III, I estimated that it now costs society—banks, check writers, and check receivers—at least $80 billion a year to write and handle about 40 billion checks a year. The adoption of EFT payment and the creation and general use of PCA will probably reduce these costs by over 80%, i/e., $64 billion.

As explained earlier, the creation of PCA will eliminate commercial banking, as well as rationalize the method of clearing payments by check or EFT. The elimination of such banking will greatly increase the revenue of the U.S. government in two ways, by shifting some $700 billion of commmercial bank assets to the government, and by enabling the government to create and spend about $20 billion of additional paper money each year (1987 figures), in both cases without any reduction in private nominal income and wealth. The shift of bank assets is worth about $42 billion a year at 6% interest. Thus the total benefit from the creation of PCA, as of 1987, would be 64, plus 42, plus 20 billion, or $126 billion, an immense sum.

3. Benefits of PCA Differ from Those of EFT

It is noteworthy that the concentration of all demand deposits and all debiting and crediting of such accounts in a single office (PCA) will yield very great economic benefits even if nearly all payments continue to be made by checks. The creation of PCA will drastically reduce check handling costs. It will radically reduce wage-payment costs because every employer will be able to send all his wage checks to a single office. It will equally reduce the costs to business firms of paying debts to suppliers because all checks will be sent to a single demand-deposit-holding agency, instead of thousands of suppliers or suppliers' banks. And the monthly payment reports submitted to depositors will be so uniform, so inclusive, and so designed that they will be far more useful to the police, the tax collector, the government statistician, and the depositor than the average bank statement now received by depositors in commercial banks.

In other words, the economic benefits which will result from the creation of PCA will be very large and will be additional to those which will result from the substitution of EFT for payment by check.

4. Possible Objections to Creation of PCA

Since no previous writer has predicted the creation of a national PCA, no objections to it have been stated, and I must try to anticipate what they may be.

(1) Too Much Concentration of Power

It will probably be objected that voters will not permit the creation of a single national payment-clearing agency because this might result in an undue concentration of economic and political power. This objection is plausible when applied to the concentration of banking, but the PCA will not be a commercial bank. It will not possess the economic and political power which naturally accrues to those who create bank money and make bank loans. PCA will merely debit and credit existing demand accounts. It will record the payments of powerful persons, but will not itself have much economic or political power.

(2) Less Loan Funds

Secondly, it may be objected that the concentration of all demand deposits in a single distant agency will make it far more difficult for local business men to borrow money in the form of new or reallocated demand deposits. But, as explained in detail in Chapter V, this is itself highly desirable for a variety of reasons. Moreover, business men will still be able to borrow money from local savings banks and from all other lending agencies except commercial banks.

(3) Distant Site of PCA

Thirdly, it may be objected that the concentration of all demand deposits in a single, centrally located PCA will remove them too far from depositors, and thus prevent quick and convenient use of such deposits. But it will take much less time for checks on such a monopoly to clear than it now takes the average check to clear because all checks drawn on PCA will be checks "on us" and will pass through only one office. Moreover, every depositor will eventually be able to use wire EFT, instead of a check, and wire EFT yields an instant debit or credit. And every neighborhood will soon have a public ATM where any depositor can obtain cash or make a deposit. Finally, each neighborhood will also have a savings bank which will provide all services previously provided by commercial banks, except the creation, holding, and servicing of demand deposits. Every former customer of a local commercial bank will still be able to rent a safety deposit box, buy an insurance policy or a government bond, make a savings deposit, borrow money, etc., at his local savings bank or some other local financial office. He will suffer no inconvenience from the elimination of local commercial banks, and will get much cheaper and faster demand-deposit debit and credit service from the new, distant national PCA.

(4) Less Urban Employment

Fourth, it may be objected that removal of demand-deposit debit-credit processing, which now requires over a million workers, from local business districts throughout the country will seriously injure such districts by reducing local payroll and rent payments, which will reduce local property values. One plausible answer to this objection is that nearly all such business districts now suffer from severe traffic congestion and/or air pollution, evils which will be reduced by the removal of one million down-town office workers. Another answer is that nearly all labor-saving inventions and procedures reduce some property values, and that this has never permanently prevented the adoption of such inventions and procedures.

(5) Monopoly Profits

It may also be objected that the creation of PCA will enable it to earn monopoly profits. The answer to this objection is that we already have many monopolies—including most public utilities—and governments have learned how to reasonably limit monopoly profits without destroying incentives to efficient operation. In nearly all such cases, the numerous economies made possible by monopoly far outweigh any inefficiency due to profit limitation.

(6) States' Rights

The states' rights argument has been repeatedly used against almost every federal reform program, from the abolition of slavery down to the creation of Medicaid and Medicare. And a conservative Supreme Court might declare that the creation of PCA is unconstitutional. But if this problem arises, it will be solved by appointing more liberal judges, and/or by amending the Constitution.

(7) Possible Use to Suppress Dissent

In their discussion of a "National Ledger Payment System," somewhat like my PCA, Ritter and Silber noted that one obvious advantage of government ownership of such a system is that the state could deny use of the system to Communists "and other malcontents," by which "the American Way of LIfe could be made even more secure" (p. 595). According to them, the U.S. has denied social security benefits to employees of the Communist Party USA for this purpose.

Most liberal Americans would consider the possibility of such use a disadvantage rather than an advantage to be gained by establishing a national PCA. However, all governments already have such immense powers to suppress dissent that any increase in such power would have little effect. Most great social reforms—the creation of public schools, the granting of old-age pensions, the provision of free health care, etc.—have increased the power of the government to suppress dissent by denying benefits to dissenters. All of these reforms were beneficial in spite of the fact that they could easily be used to suppress dissent. Therefore, the possible charge that PCA could be used to suppress dissent should not block or delay the creation of PCA.

The only effective basis for freedom of dissent in advanced countries is public opinion, general belief in such freedom. Whenever public opinion supports suppression of dissent, any government can easily suppress dissent, regardless of its constitution or laws. In 1932, Germany still had a model constitution and good laws on freedom of dissent, but these legal devices did not prevent suppression of dissent by the new Nazi rulers.

(8) Destruction of PCA Records

Finally, the concentration of all payment processing and records in a single office may seem unwise because this office could be destroyed by a single fire, nuclear bomb, or natural catastrophe. But the government could easily reconstitute the most recent data by requiring all depositors to send it copies of their most recent monthly PCA reports. Also, PCA itself could store copies of all its reports on microfilm in one or more remote storage facilities.

5. PCA Service Charges

The PCA will be largely financed by service charges per debit or credit, charges based on true marginal cost, variable cost at the margin, not on any cumulative or average cost. Any deficit due to such pricing will be met by the government out of general tax revenues.

I have stated the case for such marginal-cost pricing in several books, most notably, *Marginal-Cost Price-Output Control* (Columbia, 1956), probably the first book on such pricing, and do not wish to repeat it here. The main conclusion applicable to PCA is that rates should vary from time to time during each day, week, or month and should fall almost to zero whenever a low rate does not result in full use of the PCA wire and computer complex. Any price high enough to result in less than full use, 24 hours a day, would be grossly uneconomic.

6. Private vs Public Ownership

The problem of whether PCA will be a private or a public agency is relatively minor. Either a private or public agency could function well. Of course, in either case, the government will tightly control the creation of new demand deposits and the destruction of old ones, but the great need is for monopoly, not for government ownership and operation. In this case, as in so many others, most of the alleged benefits of socialism can be achieved by the creation of a well-regulated private monopoly.

The chief argument against private ownership is that this might prevent or delay the adoption of true marginal-cost pricing.

7. The Location of PCA

PCA will probably be located in a new planned town located on infertile farm land near an existing city close to the population center of the U.S. This will help to minimize construction costs and land rent for the new PCA plant and all other new buildings in the new satellite town. It will also help to minimize the costs of communication between deposit holders and the PCA.

8. Gradual vs Sudden Adoption of Reforms

Most of the major reforms predicted in this book will be adopted gradually over a long period, without any special one-time action by the government. But the last two reforms discussed—creation of a single check-clearing agency, and the elimination of commercial banking—will probably require radical one-time interference by the state. Private bankers will be reluctant to give up the creation of money because it is highly profitable. And the creation of a single national debit-credit payment agency will also probably require state action because it will reduce many property values and will require simultaneous action by all banks.

Both reforms should probably be adopted suddenly and simultaneously because each would facilitate the other. For instance, the concentration of all demand deposits in a single agency will both end the creation of new deposits by all other agencies, and will also minimize the costs of processing debits and credits to these depossits.

CHAPTER VII

FAR MORE USE OF PAYMENT DATA TO DETECT CRIME

1. Statement of Fifth Prediction

My fifth major forecast concerning future U.S. monetary and banking reform is that the records of debits and credits to demand-deposit accounts will be increasingly used for many decades as a means of detecting crime and prosecuting and convicting criminals. Of course, such data will also be used to defend the innocent. Such uses of payment data will be steadily improved. Their use to detect crime will soon become by far the cheapest and most effective method of detecting, and therefore preventing, crime. By the year 2100, such use, together with a 200%+ rise in real wages, will have reduced major U.S. crime rates to less than 80% of the 1986 level.

Demand-deposit debits and credits are now reported monthly to depositors in reports called bank statements. However, as explained earlier, the new monopoly (PCA), which will hold all demand deposits, will not be a commercial bank, and therefore its reports will not be called bank statements. I call them demand-deposit-use statements, or payment statements. Of course, bank statements are also payment statements.

2. Past Use of Bank Data to Detect Crime

The use of U.S. bank records by police to detect crime and catch criminals, and by prosecutors and courts to prosecute and convict persons accused of crime, has been growing for many decades, but has often been slow and difficult because Americans are permitted to have two or more bank accounts under two or more names in widely separated places, including foreign countries, and because the police must usually secure the permission of a judge to obtain or inspect bank records.

In recent years, several new state and federal banking laws designed to help the police, the FBI, and tax collectors detect major crimes have been enacted. The most important of these is the Federal Bank Secrecy Act of 1970, which requires banks to report to the Treasury all cash transactions of over $10,000. Over 70 banks have recently been fined for routinely violating this law. The Crocker National Bank of California was compelled to pay a $2.2 million fine.

On December 30, 1986, the Senate Permanent Investigating Subcommittee published a 34-page report on underworld misuse of commercial banks. The authors claimed to have uncovered proof of criminal money laundering of "enormous proportions," with $40 billion to $150 billion in drug loot alone channeled through banks which violated the Federal Bank Secrecy Act.

Senator Wm. Roth, chairman of the Subcommittee, described the Bank Secrecy Act "as one of the most effective tools in the arsenal of U.S. prosecutors," and called for random audits of banks by the Treasury Department to enforce this act. Unfortunately, criminals can easily evade the law by making deposits of $9,900 in each of many different banks. And most banks ignored the law until very recently, when the U.S. suddenly began to collect million-dollar fines from violators of this law.

3. The Reasons for My Prediction

There are several reasons why police review of all payment statements (PRPS) will be increasingly used to detect crime.

(1) The proportion of payments made by demand-deposit debits will continue to grow indefinitely

(2) The creation of PCA will greatly facilitate the use of PRPS for crime detection

(3) Public demand for more effective crime detection will continue to grow indefinitely

(4) The use of PRPS to detect crime will be far more effective and far cheaper than any alternative method of crime detection.

I shall now discuss each of these reasons separately and more fully.

(1) The Growth of Payment by Check

The proportion of payments made by check and EFT has been growing in all advanced countries for over

200 years because payment by check is usually more convenient and/or cheaper than payment in cash. Checks can be safely sent through the mail, and, when lost or stolen, they are much harder to appropriate or spend than cash. And it is much easier to write a check for a large, odd sum than to count the same sum in cash. Also, use of a check leaves a record of payment.

These advantages of payment by check or EFT will long continue to increase spontaneous use of checks and EFT. In the course of this further voluntary increase in the relative use of payment by check or EFT it will become more and more apparent that all legitimate payments can be easily made by check or EFT, and that only actual and potential criminals continue to need and demand payment in paper money. As a result, demand for increased restriction of the issue and use of paper money will continue to grow and become stronger.

In recent decades there has been an extraordinary increase in the amount of paper money in circulation in the U.S., especially in $100 bills and other high-value bills. By 1986, the total had risen to some $200 billion, from $20 billion in 1950, and $50 billion in 1970. Probably over $100 billion is in the hands of drug dealers and other criminals. The Police often find and seize millions of dollars in currency when they raid drug dealers.

Most of these illegal gains could easily be appropriated peacefully and cheaply by simply requiring all holders of $20 or higher bills to exchange this currency for demand deposits at their bank. Holders of illegal gains would be unable to justify their hoards, which should be confiscated. Many holders of legal hoards would be unable to prove that they had paid income taxes on them. Other holders should be compensated liberally for depositing their old currency.

To secure the maximum benefit from the use of PRPS to detect crimes and to catch and convict criminals, all advanced countries will increasingly restrict both their issue of paper money and the use of such money to make substantial payments. These restrictions alone will drastically reduce the volume of many crimes—drug dealing, kidnapping, bank robberies, etc.—because such crimes require the use of large sums of paper money. Few criminals can risk accepting checks or writing checks because they leave incriminating trails when processed by banks. On the other hand, honest men prefer to use checks because they leave valuable evidence of payments and receipts.

One of the first new steps in the restriction of the use of paper money will be the gradual withdrawal from circulation of all large-denomination bills. The Federal Reserve System stopped printing $500 and $1,000 bills several years ago, and it has been retiring those deposited in banks. In 1962 the Internal Revenue Service proposed the elimination of $100 bills in order to increase income-tax revenues. I predict that the printing of all bills above $10 in 1986 value will cease before 2050 A.D.

F. Lee Bailey, the famous criminal lawyer, proposed in 1981 that to receive, possess, or spend more than $500 in cash should be made illegal. "Legitimate citizens do not need to do business in cash," he said.

In addition to gradually restricting the quantity of paper money in use, all advanced countries will gradually adopt ever-more restrictions on the possession and use of cash. For instance, by 2050 A.D., the U.S. will prohibit the use of cash to pay wages, rent, and interest, and to buy any article or service worth more than $100. It will also make illegal the possession of more than $1,000 in cash by any person or firm which does not obviously need such a sum for conducting a legal business.

High-value coins could replace paper money as a means of illegal payment. Fortunately, few such coins circulate in advanced countries. To prevent any substitution of such coins for paper money, all advanced nations will soon prohibit the circulation of such coins.

Every future step in the restriction of the creation, possession, and use of paper money and high-value coins will force the public to make greater use of checks and/or EFT orders to make payments. As a result, payment statements will record an ever larger share of all monetary payments, and will therefore become ever more useful in the detection of crime and the prosecution of criminals.

(2) The Creation of PCA

As I explained in Chapter VI, the creation of a single national agency (PCA) to hold all demand deposits and clear all debits and credits to such accounts is inevitable because it will reduce the cost of such activities by over 80%, and also provide faster and superior service. It will also greatly facilitate the use of payment statements to detect crime and convict criminals.

The creation of PCA will enable all police detectives and tax collectors to obtain far more information on the income and expenses of any suspect than they could previously obtain. Moreover, such information will be obtainable from a single agency, and will be shown on standard payment statements designed to simplify the inspection of the data by computers or detectives.

The mere concentration of all demand deposits and all debiting and crediting of such deposits in a single new agency will result in the regular preparation and distribution of nationally uniform payment statements which will be far more revealing, and of far more use to the police and to tax collectors than bank statements have ever been. But other measures will be adopted to make these payment statements even more useful to the police.

At present, every American is allowed to have several different demand accounts in the U.S. and abroad, and to shift funds from one to another, often in order to confuse the police and tax collectors. To make PCA statements simpler and more revealing, the U.S. government will eventually require that each person or family use only one demand account, and that all income be directly deposited to this account.

For the same reason, it will also require that PCA payment-statement forms be so designed, and that debits and credits be entered on such forms in such a way, as to simplify and speed up police inspection of these statements, including inspection by computers. For instance, it will require that both income credits and expenditure debits be grouped by category—wages, rent or housing costs, food, etc.—and shown in the same place on every payment statement. To aid such classification, the government will require that all checks and EFT orders specify the category of the payment.

To help income-tax collectors determine personal incomes, the government will require that all personal monetary receipts which are not personal income —bequests, gifts, loan repayments, payments for assets sold, etc.—be deposited in savings accounts. and that transfers of funds from savings accounts to demand accounts be separately listed and grouped on all PCA payment statements. Such separation of income credits from other demand deposit credits will be very useful to depositors, as well as to tax collectors.

The above explanation applies primarily to personal or family payment statements, and will make it almost impossible for any individual or family to conceal illegal income and expenses, or to evade income taxes. Bank and payment statements for business firms will be far more complex, but they too will be designed and standardized by industry so as to make inspection and interpretation of them as easy and revealing as possible. Moreover, the government will prohibit the use of business and government funds to pay personal and family living costs. It will require that all business payments to persons and families—wages, dividends, interest, etc.—pass through personal or family accounts before being spent. Thus, illegal gains by business firms will not benefit individuals unless shown on personal payment statements.

The PCA will send copies of all payment statements to both the national police headquarters and to local police departments, as well as to all demand depositors. Preliminary police inspection of these statements will be done by computers programmed to pick out all statements which include significant changes in personal income or expenses, or items related to suspicious entries in other payment statements. It may be possible to use for such review the same PCA computers used to prepare payment statements.

(3) Growing Demand for Effective Crime Detection

The third major reason why the use of payment statements to detect crime and convict criminals will increase greatly and become routine is that public demand for effective crime detection and prevention has long been growing, and will continue to grow indefinitely in advanced countries. Every increase in the average wealth of individuals increases the opportunity for theft, burglary, fraud, etc., and also increases public demand for protection. Every improvement in the means of travel helps criminals to escape from the scene of the crime more rapidly, and to evade pursuers more successfully. Every increase in the effectiveness and portability of hand guns and small bombs makes terrorism more common and more frightening.

Most crime rates have more than doubled in the U.S. in the last 30 years, and they may continue to rise in the U.S. and other countries for some time. But the public demand for protection against crime is very likely to continue to grow, even if crime rates do not continue to rise, because the standard of living will continue to rise, which will increase both the ability to pay for crime protection and the demand for it. In economic terms, the demand for crime protection is highly elastic.

(4) The Benefits of Police Review of Payments

The fourth and most important reason why all advanced countries will eventually make payment statements more comprehensive and informative, and make PRPS routine, is simply that it is already obvious that such measures will be highly effective, both in reducing the volume of crime and in reducing the cost of crime prevention and detection. This claim can be supported both by general arguments and by considering individual classes of crime.

i. General Benefits

When every person is required to receive nearly all income as direct deposits to his one demand account with PCA, and to pay for all significant purchases (over $10?) with debits to this account, his monthly payment statement will be highly revealing. It will be almost impossible for him to hide any illegal income or illegal payment. And, if he does receive and try to hide any illegal income, the police will be able to trace the source of it by inspecting the debits and credits which created this income.

Police review of comprehensive payment statements will be highly effective and increasingly acceptable because the new and improved payment statements will make it cheap and easy to detect most crimes without dangerous and costly detective work, raids on criminal hangouts, and pursuit of fleeing suspects. Computers, which become cheaper every year, will largely replace detectives, whose pay ought to rise each year. Automation of police work will be as productive as automation of factories has been. Moreover, the need for jails and prisons will decline by over 50% because convicts will be unable to evade fines, and prison escapees will be unable to write checks and pay their living costs. The growing use of fines will, in time, largely replace imprisonment as an effective method of punishment, and will permit ever more liberal compensation payments to victims of crime.

Income from crime is usually irregular and abnormal in amount, which is one reason why it is easy to detect when reported on payment statements. Moreover, the sources of such income are also abnormal, which has the same effect. And, if the police learn that one man has an illegal income from one source, they will check all payments from this source to other payees. Payment records are especially useful in crime detection because they always reveal both the recipient and the source of any illegal income. Detection of an illegal payment always permits detection of an illegal payor, and vice versa.

Moreover, the evidence of crime revealed in payment records is permanent. It may be discovered and used many years after the crime was committed.

As previously noted, the mere elimination of high-denomination paper money will radically reduce the amount of crime because potential criminals are well aware that illegal income in the form of checks and EFT is far easier to detect than illegal cash income. The public announcement that all payment statements will be routinely inspected by police and tax collectors will markedly enhance or supplement this desirable effect on the volume of crime. The resulting radical reduction in crime rates will sharply lower the need for actual police inspection of payment records, which, in turn will equally reduce the cost of such inspection, perhaps by over 80%.

In America the chance that the perpetrator of any specific crime, murder excepted, will be arrested and convicted is less than 10%. That is why most criminals believe that crime pays, at least until they have received a long prison sentence. Any measure which makes punishment for crime more certain tends to reduce the amount of crime. Since PRPS will make arrest and conviction far more certain, it will greatly reduce crime rates.

Having stated the major general reasons why PRPS will be highly effective as a means of preventing and detecting crime, and as an aid to prosecutors of indicted criminals, I turn now to an explanation of the effects of PRPS on individual classes of crime.

ii. The Effects of PRPS on Individual Classes of Crime

(i) Robbery and Theft

Bank robberies and thefts will virtually cease for two chief reasons. First, the cash stolen will not be spendable, except on very minor retail items. Bank robbers and thieves will not be able to use stolen money to pay rent, buy a car, purchase new clothing, buy a week's groceries, and so forth.

Secondly, banks will hold less than 10% as much paper money as they now hold, and all of it will be in $1 and $5 bills. Criminals will find it difficult to steal, carry, and conceal large amounts of such bills.

When individuals are required to make all substantial payments by check or EFT, they will carry very little cash on their person. As a result, hold-ups and muggings will become far less profitable. Moreover, the little cash obtained will be far more difficult to spend. It follows that the number of robberies will decline drastically, probably by over 80%.

Burglary also will decline about as much for similar reasons. People will keep far less cash in their homes. And stolen goods will rarely be saleable because potential buyers will not have much cash, and will be very reluctant to write checks to pay for stolen goods. If burglars or robbers do accept checks and deposit them in their personal bank accounts, such deposits will be very likely to attract police attention and investigation, and criminals will find it hard to explain the origin of the cash deposited.

About a million autos are stolen each year in the U.S. A large proportion are stolen for joy rides, and are recovered by the owners. PRPS will not reduce such thefts. But it will virtually end the theft of autos for resale or breakup because few potentionl buyers will be able to pay cash, and payment by check or EFT will leave records readily availble to the police. Moreover, auto thieves will not be able to use cash obtained by selling stolen cars or parts to pay their own major living costs.

(ii) Political Corruption

Political corruption is widespread in the U.S. In March, 1978, a former member of Congress was accused of accepting about $250,000 from agents of the South Korean government, and other Congressmen accepted smaller amounts from this source, largely in cash. Political corruption usually involves cash payments because bank debits leave evidence. When cash ceases to be legal tender for large payments, those who want to bribe public officials will be unable to raise large sums of cash, and public officials will no longer be able to spend cash bribes for living expenses or luxuries. As a result, political corruption will largely disappear.

(iii) Illegal Drug Use

Illegal trade in narcotics, tobacco, and hard liquor is now almost entirely financed by large sums of cash. If drug dealers and bootleggers could not obtain large sums of cash, could not deposit their cash profits in banks, and could not pay cash for any item costing more than a very small sum, nearly all dealers in illegal goods would change their occupation. And the costly and ineffective methods now used to check such trade could be abandoned.

The Research Triangle Institute has estimated that illegal drug use cost the U.S. economy $60 billion in 1983. Other estimates rise to $150 billion for 1986. Drug abusers are far less productive than their co-workers, miss ten times as many workdays, and are three times as likely to injure themselves. Moreover, addicts are far more likely to rob, to steal, and to mug old people on the street.

The recent unexpected and unprecedented efforts to vigorously enforce the Bank Secrecy Act (BSA), which requires banks to report cash deposits of $10,000 or more, seems to have made some drug smugglers desperate and reckless. In June, 1987, FBI agents, pretending to be money launderers, were able to entrap 91 cocaine dealers by laundering $150 million of their profits. The FBI confiscated $20 million in cash and 2100 pounds of cocaine with a wholesale value of $28 million (<u>S.F.Chronicle</u>, 6-11-87; p. 54).

The BSA is a very small step towards the routine police review of payment statements (PRPS) advocated in this chapter. Full use of PRPS would be over ten times as effective as the use of the BSA in reducing the volume of drug dealing.

In a June 30, 1987, radio address to a national audience, N.Y. City District Attorney Juliani, the highly successful prosecutor of Mafia leaders and drug dealers, proposed five methods of improving crime prevention, all of which have long been used, with little success. He did not suggest any reduction in the circulation of currency or any increase in police inspection of bank statements.

(iv) Illegal High-Stake Gambling

In 1967 a Presidential Commission on Law Enforcement and the Administration of Justice estimated that the total national economic cost of crime and government administration of justice amounted to about 3% of U.S. GNP, of which about one-third was due to illegal gambling. This implies that the total monetary cost of gambling, the chief source of income and power for the Mafia, was about $80 billion in 1986. The total social cost was much larger because gambling losses caused many large thefts and embezzlements, and resulted in many divorces, and much worry, sickness, and suicide.

Operators of illegal gambling houses will no longer accept checks after the police begin to inspect bank statements. And would-be gamblers will not be able to assemble large cash funds for gambling, or to spend large cash winnings. As a result, illegal gambling for large stakes will virtually cease. And this benefit will be achieved while spending on law enforcement is being radically reduced.

(v) Tax Evasion

If no person had more than one checking account and nearly all his income and outlay passed through that account, it would be impossible for any person to hide any significant part of his income from income-tax collectors, who could collect the proper tax by directly debiting his demand deposit. PRPS would virtually end income-tax evasion and cheating, and would radically reduce income-tax collection costs. Moreover, if income-tax deductions were ended, as they should be, it would be possible to free taxpayers from the often onerous task of preparing and submitting annual income-tax forms. Of course, income-tax collectors might need some additional information—age, marital status, number of children, etc.—but the cost of obtaining or providing such data would be very small.

Estimates of the amount of income-tax revenue lost due to tax evasion and cheating vary widely. One estimate is that about 25% of all U.S. economic activity is underground and unreported to tax collectors. Such activity includes not only illegal activities like prostitution, drug dealing, gambling, etc., but also includes much relatively legitimate activity such as unreported repair work, construction, health care, barter, etc. In 1987, U.S. GNP was about $4 trillion, which implies tht the underground economy produced about $1 trillion of unreported income, and that failure to report this income cost the Internal Revenue Service over $100 billion. The IRS has estimated that this revenue loss rose from $82 billion in 1981 to $103 billion in 1986.

In 1986 the IRS spent $4.8 billion collecting federal taxes. Since state and local government revenue is almost as large as federal revenue, I estimate total 1986 U.S. tax-collection costs at $9.0 bil. The creation of PCA and the use of PRPS to determine tax liabilities will reduce U.S. tax-collection costs by over 50%, in addition to increasing taxes due by over $100 billion (as of 1986). And it will sharply reduce the heavy cost to taxpayers of preparing income and sales-tax returns.

Effective, uniform enforcement of income-tax laws will greatly reduce public dissatisfaction with tax laws because taxpayers will become much more confident that other persons are paying their proper taxes in full. Moreover, the tax burden on honest taxpayers will be reduced by improved enforcement of tax laws.

(vi) White Collar Crime

According to investigators working for Representative Douglas Boyd, Jr. (D-GA), fraud at S&Ls has "reached epidemic proportions" and was involved in most of California's 31 thrift failures over the past three years and was responsible for a large share of the $3.7 billion losses (S.F. Chronicle, 6-13-87; p. 54). Figures for the entire U.S. would be about three times as large. Losses from fraud by commercial bank employees may be even larger.

Estimates of the sum required to pay off depositors in all insolvent U.S. S&Ls now range from $25 to $100 billion, of which about 15% is the result of fraud by S&L executives (S.F. Examiner, 6-28-87; p. D1).

The U.S. Commerce Department has estimated that white collar crime, mostly embezzlement, costs U.S. business $40 to $50 billion a year. For instance, bank employees get away with far more bank money than do bank robbers. This is possible only because bank employees can steal cash, or can write checks convertible into large amounts of cash. This will be impossible when the use of cash has been virtually ended.

Many purchasing-department executives have induced suppliers to grant rebates, payable to these executives, in return for profitable orders. When all large payments must be made by check or EFT, suppliers will be unable to make such rebates without leaving clear evidence of fraud in both the supplier's and the purchasing agent's payment records.

(vii) Illegal Immigration

The adoption of PRPS will make it possible both

to prevent nearly all illegal immigration into the U.S. and to spend much less money on finding and deporting illegal aliens. Such aliens will not be able to have demand accounts and receive wage payments because all wages will have to be paid directly into checking accounts, and aliens will not be able to spend any cash illegally obtained. Legal immigrants will of course be given U.S. demand accounts upon proof of their legal entry. Under this system no border fences, immigration patrols, or airport immigration agents will be needed to prevent illegal immigration. It will no longer be necessary to enter and search private homes and businesses, and insult naturalized citizens by stopping and checking them on the street, in order to catch and deport illegal aliens.

The inducement to the citizens of poor countries to emigrate, legally or illegally, to some rich country will be very great as long as international differences in average wages remain high, and this condition is likely to continue for centuries. Moreover, travel costs will continue to fall indefinitely. Hence, all rich countries will long continue to need effective and economical methods of preventing illegal immigration.

The social costs of illegal immigration are very high. It increases the supply of labor, and therefore causes unemployment, and reduces wage rates relatively, especially the wage rates of the worst-paid workers. Immigrants occupy scarce low-rent housing badly needed by our homeless. They overcrowd our schools, hospitals, and jails. The adoption of PRPS will virtually end illegal immigration and these and other large social costs of such immigration.

(viii) Terrorism

Terrorism has been growing in Europe and America for several decades, and will probably continue to grow. Moreover, within a decade or two, terrorists are likely to secure small atomic bombs, which will greatly increase the danger they pose, and will justify far more vigorous efforts to limit terrorism. Since effective organized terrorists cannot operate without very substantial financial support, limitation of the use of cash and continuous police review of payment statements may soon become essential elements of any effective anti-terrorist program. And any further intensification of terrorism will reduce opposition to the invasion of privacy involved in PRPS. The explosion of the first nuclear bomb by terrorists will greatly increase public demand for PRPS.

(ix) Confidence Tricks

Almost every day, U.S. newspapers report cases of confidence tricks which may have cost the victim his life savings. For instance, professional con men have persuaded many partially senile senior citizens to withdraw their bank deposits in cash and entrust them to the con men for a few minutes or hours in order to enable the trickster, who claims to be an FBI man, to test the honesty of some bank cashier or officer. After the pseudo test, of course, the victim is repaid with wads of waste paper rather than cash. Such confidence games would cease if depositors were no longer able to withdraw their deposits in cash, and if con men could no longer use cash to pay for their living costs.

(x) Other Crimes

Losses from counterfeiting are small compared with losses from other crimes discussed here, but it may be worth noting that they would cease if no paper money but $1 and $5 bills were printed. It is not now profitable to counterfeit small change or one-dollar bills, and it would become much less profitable if counterfeiters could not deposit such bills, in their personal bank accounts or use them for large purchases.

Kidnapping is not common in America, but it has become a serious problem in some European countries. In 1977, kidnappers collected some $250,000,000 in ransom money in Italy. If kidnappers suddenly learned that the families of their victims could no longer raise large cash ransom payments, and that cash ransom payments could no longer be spent for most living costs and luxuries, they would cease their kidnapping. Some kidnapping, of course, is political, but it is relatively insignificant. Moreover, it is costly to finance, and would be greatly hindered by the reform proposed here.

The volume of prostitution will be drastically reduced because prostitutes and pimps will not be able to deposit or spend large cash incomes. Customers may still be able to make small cash payments, or give valuables, to prostitutes, but the latter will be unable to use such income to pay rent, to buy furniture, or make any other substantial payments.

Advanced countries now employ thousands of

customs agents to inspect the handbags and luggage of international travelers. It will be far cheaper and more effective to inspect the demand deposits and credits of suspected smugglers than to inspect their baggage and freight shipments. Moreover, no traveler will be able to sell any valuable goods for cash, or to take cash out of the country. The adoption of these measures will drastically reduce the volume of smuggling in any advanced country, will make the hiring of customs agents unnecessary, and will make foreign travel more rapid and pleasant for all tourists.

Many other ways in which PRPS will reduce crime and corruption might be noted, but the above illustrations should suffice to show how effective it will be.

In spite of the high costs of crime, there has been little if any discussion of the crime-prevention reforms advocated in this book. The only previous discussion I am aware of is that contained in the utopian novel Freeland, published by the Austrian economist Theodore Hertzka in 1890.

iii. The Effect on Prison and Police Costs

American prisons and jails now hold about 500,000 inmates. If holding an inmate costs on average $10,000 a year, a conservative estimate, the total cost of keeping these inmates is $5 billion a year. Moreover, if these inmates were free and employed, they would earn about $10,000 a year, so the total cost to society of keeping them in prison is about $10 billion a year. And, if they were free and employed, their mental and physical health would be better, and their lives would be much more pleasant and satisfying.

Creation of PCA and PRPS will reduce the U.S. jail and prison population by 60 to 80% for three reasons. First, it will radically increase the percentage of crimes which are detected and proven in court. Nothing deters crime more than a high probability of detection and punishment. At present, this probability is very low in the U.S., well below 5%, and potential criminals are well aware that this rate is very low. Adoption of the predicted new methods of crime-detection will increase this rate above 80%, which will radically reduce the number of crimes and therefore the number of convicts.

Secondly, adoption of the proposed methods of crime control will eventually make it possible to punish most criminals without imprisoning them.

Since all personal income will pass through a single agency, PCA, the government will be able to punish more and more criminals adequately by imposing fines or life-time income cuts. This system of punishment will become more feasible and effective each year as the average real income of Americans continues to rise. It has risen 300% since 1900, and will probably rise another 300% before the year 2100. Moreover, the U.S. government will soon guarantee a minimum real income, well above bare subsistence level, for all needy Americans. It will also soon provide free health care for all. These changes will make it more feasible for the government to use fines to punish the poorest criminals. The chief reason it has long been impractical to substitute fines for imprisonment as punishment for crime is that the great majority of convicts have been penniless, and have had poor employment prospects.

Of course, it will always be necesssary to imprison violent chronic criminals in order to protect the public from violence. But they make up less than 10% of our jail and prison population.

Thirdly, the requirement that all large personal purchases be paid for by debits to personal checking accounts will make it impossible for escaped convicts to live outside prison. They will be able to steal cash, but will not be able to use it to pay for housing, food, clothing, cars, etc. Knowing this, very few convicts will try to escape. As a result, prisons will not need to be escape-proof, the number of prison guards per 1000 prisoners will be drastically reduced, and it will become much easier to provide useful work for prisoners outside prison.

Over one million persons were employed as police personnel in the U.S. in 1986, and an almost equal number as private watchmen and guards. The total cost of public and private police protection was about $40 billion. The adoption of my predicted crime-reduction methods will probably reduce such costs by over 60%. All the previously explained reasons for a reduction in the volume and cost of individual crime apply here also.

iv. Total Economic Benefits of PRPS

In my review of the effects of PCA and PRPS on individual kinds of crime, I have offered some estimates of economic benefits: (1) illegal drug trade, $60 to $150 billion, (2) illegal gambling, $80 billion, (3) tax evasions, $100 billion, (4) white-collar crime, $40 billion, and (5) police and prison costs, $24 billion. The possible economic benefits from reduction in the volume of other crimes was not estimated.

In 1967 a Presidential Commission estimated the total national economic cost of crime, crime prevention, and criminal justice at about 3% of U.S. GNP, or about $150 billion in 1987. I believe that this was a gross underestimate, but it permits a minimum estimate of the total U.S. economic benefit from the adoption of PRPS, which should cut crime costs by over 67%, or about $100 billion.

(6) Effect on Psychological Costs of Crime

In addition to the economic costs of crime, of police work, of criminal courts, and of jails and prisons, there are very important psychological costs of crime. Every crime report in the newspapers or over the air causes millions of people to worry about their own safety, and that of their friends and relatives. Every victim of a violent or costly crime suffers serious psychological costs, costs which may be much more injurious to the victim than his property loss. Victims of medical malpractice or harmful industrial practices may be awarded damages for psychological suffering much larger than those awarded for economic cost or loss. It is possible that the psychological cost of living in a crime-ridden society is greater than the economic cost of crime.

(7) Effects on Consumption of Alcohol and Tobacco

The chief benefit from the application of the coming new system of crime prevention and detection will be a very great, over 80%, reduction in the physical volume of harmful drug use in the U.S., at a negligible cost. The success of this anti-drug campaign will eventually result in the adoption of severe laws against the use of alcoholic drinks and tobacco. Americans abandoned prohibition of alcoholic drinks in 1933 because they had been unable to enforce prohibition. When they learn from experience that the predicted new law-enforcement methods will work, they will reconsider the case for prohibition of alcoholic drinks, and will re-impose such prohibition. They will also prohibit the production, sale, and consumption of tobacco. These new prohibition programs will save over 160,000 U.S. lives a year, and will probably increase real GNP by over 2% ($80 billion as of 1987). They will also make the average human life happier, as well as longer and more productive.

4. Objections Answered

Since there has been little if any discussion of my predicted system of crime detection, and none known to me, it is hard to determine the chief objections to it. But I shall try nevertheless to anticipate and answer them.

(1) Reform Will Be Difficult and Costly

Perhaps the chief possible objection is that this reform will require extensive and costly changes in customary business and government practices. The main answer to this objection is that the benefits described above will more than compensate for these costs. But some further comments are in order.

Most Americans have already adopted voluntarily the use of personal checking accounts because the purely personal benefits outweigh the costs. Money in a bank account cannot be lost, stolen, or burned up. Moreover, a cashed check serves as a receipt, and bank statements are useful records. Hence, the number of people who voluntarily establish and use personal checking accounts will continue to grow until nearly all persons in advanced countries have them. It follows that a law requiring all persons to have and use such accounts would impose few if any net personal real costs. The new depositors as a group will obtain direct personal benefits outweighing the personal costs. And all the beneficial effects on crime and law enforcement will be a net social gain, a costless external economy.

Moreover, it will cost far less to detect and prevent crime by checking payment statements than by hiring police patrolmen and detectives, pursuing criminals in flight, making dangerous drug buys, raiding the homes of drug dealers, etc. Few if any police will be injured or killed while checking payment statements. Known criminls and escaped convicts will not have to be pursued because they will be unable to survive outside prison without demand deposit accounts. The denial of such accounts will be cheap and easy.

(2) More Bad Check Losses

A second possible objection to compulsory, near-universal use of bank debits as means of payment is that this will greatly increase business losses from bad checks. But many ways to reduce such losses are already available, for instance, requiring fingerprints on checks offered by unknown customers. It is now possible to obtain fingerprints quickly without soiling the fingers. Merchants do not now like to request fingerprints because they fear that honest customers will object. But, if merchants were required by law to accept all checks and to fingerprint all unknown customers, the customers could not blame the merchant and take their business to a less demanding store. Moreover, wire EFT will gradually replace payment by check, and it assures instant payment.

Finally, general use of bank identity cards and check forms containing data about the legitimate user will make it much easier for merchants to reduce bad check losses. And no merchant will be allowed to cash checks for customers. They will only accept checks for merchandise.

(3) Danger of Police State

Whenever a proposal is made to increase the range of police activities or to make police work more effective, some critic is sure to criticize it as a step towards a "police state." The term police state is so vague that it is almost meaningless, but it is meant to be pejorative. However, epithets do not change the objects to which they are applied, and their use does not contribute to rational discussion.

Like nearly all other efficiency measures, police inspection of improved payment statements could be used for good or bad purposes. But there is no sound reason to anticipate that they will be chiefly used for bad purposes. If there were, all other inventions and reforms which make government more efficient would be harmful.

Although the adoption and effective administration of the coming ideal national payment system will enable police and courts to detect, and therefore promptly penalize, over 80% of all crimes, this system will not help the government to do many of the worst things which tyrannical governments have often tried to do. It will not help the police or government officials determine the unpopular or disapproved political or religious opinions of citizens, unless the latter make large payments to agencies advocating such opinions. It will not help police determine the sexual orientation or practices of citizens, unless the latter result in large suspicious payments. In these respects, it will be far less useful to thought controllers than current U.S. loyalty investigations are.

The fact that some bad governments have had efficient police forces does not prove that good governments should have inefficient police forces. Bad governments also use the telephone, the radio, and television to control and exploit their subjects, but no one has yet argued that, for this reason, good governments should do without them.

One of the arguments for the overthrow of democratic governments most frequently used by fascists and ambitious political generals is that these governments have failed to enforce the law and control crime. Thus, any reform which helps democratic governments enforce criminal laws should reduce the danger of their overthrow by antidemocratic parties and military officers.

It is especially noteworthy that the crime-prevention effect of PRPS will be so great that this reform will radically reduce the extent of necessary police control and investigation of personal behavior. When criminals know that they can rarely benefit financially from crime, they will have far less inducement to commit crimes. And when police can catch most criminals by merely checking their bank statements, they can cease most of their other, more intrusive, crime investigation activities.

(4) Incapacity of Some Persons

It may be objected that many persons are unfit to hold and properly use demand-deposit accounts because they are illiterate, feeble-minded, senile, blind, drug-addicted, or otherwise handicaped. However, such persons find it difficult to handle cash, as well as demand deposits. Many such people should live in institutions, or should have guardians to control their spending, whether they use cash or checks. The requirement that they hold demand deposits and pay by EFT or check will create no significant new problems. Rather, it will enable guardians to monitor and control the spending of their wards, much more easily because the PCA will provide an accurate record of the income and spending of their wards.

(5) The Privacy Argument

It has been claimed that the use of bank or payment data to prevent and detect major crimes would be an immoral or illegal invasion of personal privacy, one so serious that the American people will never tolerate it. This argument has been repeatedly used against progressive social reforms such as the adoption of the income tax, the inheritance tax, the social security system, compulsory education, compulsory vaccination, etc. Since such use failed to prevent the adoption of these great reforms, it may delay, but it will not prevent, the proper use of bank or payment statements to prevent and detect crimes.

Nearly all criminal investigations and trials now result in repeated painful violations of privacy by detectives, prosecutors, and defense lawyers. Innocent witnesses, as well as defendants, are often offended by such invasions, but this has rarely been considered justification for prohibiting such invasions. There is little reason to believe that the use of PCA data on personal income and expense will substantially increase or intensify such invasion of privacy. Indeed, the use of such data may make detectives and courts so much more efficient, and crime therefore so much less common, that invasion of privacy by police and lawyers may become much less common. Moreover, the harm done by such invasion of privacy can be greatly reduced by prohibiting the news media from publicizing such invasions.

A loyalty investigation usually involves direct personal questioning of the suspect, his relatives, his neighbors, his employer, etc., and makes most of those interviewed suspicious of the suspect. The coming review of payment data will rarely require such personal interviewing. Even the review of bank statements will be largely carried out by computers, which will call attention only to obvious and serious evidence of illegal payments. Personal questioning will be justified only in those few cases where relatively convincing evidence of crime has been found by computers.

It is noteworthy that most of the conservatives who have used the privacy argument against so many beneficial social reforms did not use it against Senator McCarthy and his supporters, who carried on a national inquisition into the political opinions, personal associations, and sexual behavior of American liberals and radicals. Nor do they now protest the loyalty checks on millions of applicants for jobs in the U.S. government and in defense industries, checks which, on the whole, have resulted in no significant effects on harmful or illegal behavior. In sharp contrast, the predicted use of bank or payment data will result in a drastic reduction in the number of most crimes.

One major reason for the widespread demand for personal privacy is that many laws now permit or require unpopular invasions of privacy. For instance, most laws against abortion, birth control, sodomy, prostitution, pornography, atheism, communism, anarchism, sedition, etc., permit or require gross invasion of privacy. But the solution is to repeal or revise these laws so that they do not cause such invasion, not to weaken all law enforcement.

Nearly all crimes against individuals involve an invasion of privacy, and violent crimes--rape, kidnapping, mugging, etc.--are very serious and painful invasions of privacy. Therefore, by reducing crime, the use of payment records will reduce total invasion of privacy, especially the most serious and painful invasions of privacy.

Finally, I expect that some critics will strongly object to the use of PCA and PRPS as means of crime prevention because they believe that the best way to prevent crime is to put much greater effort on teaching ethical values and/or religious dogmas concerning the punishment of criminals after death. These critics would be unhappy if experience proves that the state can radically reduce crime by purely secular, scientific measures. Many similar critics long rejected the use of medical science to improve health because they wanted us to rely instead on prayer and religious faith.

I will not try to answer such critics here because I have repeatedly done so elsewhere. I will only note that their opposition to the use of medical science has not prevented an immense growth of such use in all advanced countries.

CHAPTER VIII. PRICE-LEVEL STABILIZATION

My sixth and last major prediction concerning the future of money and banking is that, after the elimination of commercial banking, the function of creating new money will be assigned to a National Monetary Agency (NMA) which will be instructed by Congress to stabilize some national price level, probably, the price level of consumer's goods.

My discussion of this prediction is brief because many economists have recognized the need for price-level stabilization, and many competent discussions of this need, and of various possible methods of achieving such stabilization, have been published. I believe that several of these methods would work reasonably well and I have no important new ideas on the subject.

Nevertheless, I consider it necessary to explain how the price level can, and probably will be, stabilized because I have argued that one of the two chief reasons why commercial banking will be ended is that such banking causes wide price level fluctuations, which cause immense economic losses and great human suffering. If price level stabilization is impossible, the case against commercial banking is much less strong than I have claimed it to be.

1. The Need for Price-Level Stabilization

The most general argument in favor of stabilizing some price level is that both inflation and deflation make all business and economic welfare calculation more difficult and more liable to serious error. This very general argument can be broken down into four major, but less general, arguments.

First, price-level stabilization helps producers of price goods to decide correctly what goods to produce, and how much of each to produce. It enables them to measure marginal costs, and marginal profits and losses, more accurately. When the price level of finished goods rises, the prices of different goods rise unequally, and producers' profits are affected unequally, but the changes in profits do not measure changes in real demand or need. Moreover, a general rise in profits induces most producers to increase their outputs unduly. In other words, inflation usually causes an uneconomic business boom and overinvestment. Conversely, when this price level falls, prices and profits fall unequally and uneconomically, and a harmful business recession occurs.

Secondly, both inflation and deflation make it much harder for producers to choose the most efficient methods of production. General price changes change different costs by different percentages, but the resulting cost changes do not measure real cost changes, and their use makes factor combination less efficient. Moreover, it is much more difficult for managers to determine and use costs to control output when nearly all costs are changing at different rates.

Thirdly, price-level stabilization permits economists, government officials, historians, and others to use historical statistics on wages, national income, and other important economic phenomena without laboriously adjusting the data for relevant inflation or deflation. Men have often drawn incorrect conclusions from such statistics because they have failed to adjust for relevant price-level changes, or because their adjustment has been faulty.

Fourth, inflation and deflation make it far more difficult for consumers to choose wisely among different products and to buy the ideal quantity of each good. To buy wisely and limit consumption properly, consumers must note and remember all relevant prices and price changes. Inflation and deflation not only increase greatly the number and degree of individual price changes, but also make it harder to react properly to these changes. Each price must be corrected for the change in the price level before consumers can react wisely to it.

Finally, price-level stabilization helps workers to determine when their real wages have fallen or risen, and to respond properly to nominal wage-rate changes. In the past, workers have often confused an increase in money wages with an increase in real wages. Wage rates have frequently failed to rise as fast as the cost of living, and workers have often been unaware of this. Moreover, during periods of inflation or deflation it is much harder for workers to choose wisely among jobs paying different wage rates because the rates change unequally and much more often.

When interviewed by Business Week (6-15-87), Alan Greenspan said "I have a suspicion that...we allowed more monetary expansion than was appropriate" in recent years. This remark suggests that the mere fact of inflation does not prove that too much money was created. Like Volker and other previous members of the Federal Reserve Board, Greenspan apparently does not accept the vital principal that ought to govern the creation and destruction of money, namely that all inflations and deflations are convincing evidence of bad control of the quantity of money. Inflation did continue during the period he considered, and this trend proved beyond a reasonable doubt that, as Greenspan suspected, "we allowed more monetary expansion than was appropriate."

2. Which Price Level Will be Stabilized?

The stabilization of any general price level will yield great economic benefits because it will greatly reduce fluctuations in all other general price levels. But the new price-level-stabilization agency will probably choose to stabilize the retail price level for consumers' goods.

The stabilization of different general price levels yields different social benefits. The stabilization of producers' cost prices would be especially beneficial to producers of raw materials and capital goods. The stabilization of wholesale prices of finished goods would be especially helpful to producers and wholesalers of such goods. The stabilization of retail prices, including housing rentals, would be most helpful to retailers, retail customers, and workers.

Since retail customers and workers are far more numerous than any alternative group of possible beneficiaries from price-level stabilization, and are also the least economically sophisticated, the NMA will probably choose to stabilize the level of retail prices for consumers' goods. Business firms employ accountants and managers sophisticated enough to adjust prices, costs, income, etc., for inflation or deflation, but most workers and retail customers are much less competent to do this. Therefore, it is more desirable to stabilize the prices that affect them most often and most directly than to stabilize any other price level.

If the retail price level for consumers' goods is stabilized, wage rates will rise steadily as real output per worker increases. It is much better to have wage rates rise, than to have wholesale and retail prices fall, as production becomes more efficient because declines in wholesale and retail prices reduce profits and production. Moreover, workers are more aware of, and more pleased by, wage raises than by equal cuts in retail prices, which they usually underestimate.

3. How the Price Level Will be Stabilized

(1) The Equation of Exchange

The so-called "equation of exchange," MxV=PxT, states clearly and concisely the most important of all monetary theories. In this equation, M is the quantity of money, V is the average velocity of circulation of money, P is the price level and T is the total number of monetary transactions. The equation makes clear that the price level is directly determined by three factors only, which implies that to control P one must control M, V, or T. Both V and T are largely determined by the private decisions of millions of individuals, and, therefore, any national government would find it impossible to control P by controlling them. But any government can easily control P by controlling M. To do this, it must prohibit private creation of money. It can then regulate the creation of money so as to prevent both inflation and deflation.

Over the past 35 years the velocity of circulation of money (V) has risen at an average rate of about 3.3%. But in the third quarter of 1979 it began to fall and during the next seven years it fell at an average rate of about 1% a year. Such fluctuations do not make it difficult to control P by regulating M because it is easy to allow for and offset any change in V by an offsetting change in M. Moreover, it is not essential to know how V is changing. All the creator of money needs to know is the effect of his actions on P, and this can always be directly observed.

(2) The Continuous Need for New Money

In a growing economy, some new money must be created each year to allow for an increase in output (T) to occur without any resulting deflation (decline in P). Fortunately, P is normally almost stable, especially in any short period, so the effect of a change in M or T falls almost entirely on P.

Whenever P begins to rise, NMA will try to

reverse the rise by reducing the rate at which it creates and issues new money. If its first effort does not quickly reverse the rise, it should take stronger measures, even including a reduction in M, until it has restored P to its previous level. Whenever P begins to fall, the NMA will increase the rate at which it creates and issues new money, and should continue to do so until P has returned to its previous level. If NMA observes P constantly, and if it acts promptly, it should learn how to prevent fluctuations in P of more than 1% in either direction.

(3) Definition of M

It has been claimed that the sort of price-level control predicted here will not work because the term <u>money</u> cannot be precisely defined. And the recent U.S. legalization of checks drawn on savings accounts, brokerage accounts, and other nonbank accounts makes this claim more plausible than ever.

It was long customary to use M1, originally defined as the sum of demand deposits and cash in circulation, as the best measure of money in discussions of the effect of changes in the quantity of money on price. Unfortunately, M1 has been redefined to include some negotiable time deposits, and M1A has been used to mean what M1 originally meant.

During the four years from 7-1-81 to 6-30-85, M1A grew by about 20%, and M1 (which includes M1A plus NOW and Super-NOW deposits) grew by about 40%. Since consumers' prices rose only about 17%, it is clear that the growth of NOW deposits (interest-bearing negotiable time deposits) had far less effect upon price levels than did the growth of demand deposits (<u>NewsWeek</u>, 12-9-85, p. 48).

Since both NOW deposits and demand deposits are now means of payment, and since both pay interest, it is difficult to explain this difference. It may be a case of cultural lag. People have long been accustomed to pay bills with checks on demand deposits, but have not yet learned to do so by drawing on NOW deposits. Or they may be reluctant to give up their NOW deposits because they earn higher rates of interest.

There is a very easy and sound solution to the problem of how to define and measure M. We need only define money as cash and demand deposits.

To simplify the problem of defining and measuring M, and the task of controlling the quantity of money in use in the U.S., the federal government will eventually prohibit the creation and use of money and money substitutes—credit cards, debit cards, coupons, tokens, notes due, warehouse receipts, credit balances, negotiable time deposits, etc.—by all private firms, and by all government agencies except the new national monetary agency (NMA) entrusted with this function.

To further simplify these two problems, the U.S. government will also prohibit the use of foreign money, including Eurodollars, to make payments within the U.S. For the same reasons, NMA will end the practice of requiring depositors to maintain minimum balances in their deposits.

In sum, the best way to solve the problem of defining money is to prohibit the creation and use of all means of payment except demand deposits, coins, and paper money, and to define the supply of money as the sum of these three kinds of money. This prohibition will create no significant social costs, and will yield a significant social benefit, better control of the chosen price level.

(4) Eurodollars

One of the most unexpected and surprising monetary developments since 1945 has been the rapid growth in the volume of dollar demand deposits in foreign, mostly European, commercial and central banks, the so-called Eurodollars.

According to Thomas J. Peters,

> "Eurodollar holdings—footloose American dollars deposited in unregulated European money-center banks—have soared to $1 trillion, three times more than the reserves held by the U.S. Treasury. This 'hot money' obliterates national borders and wreaks havoc with government policies as it flits around the globe at, literally, the speed of light—thanks to modern electronic banking—in search of the next set of financing opportunities: junk-bond-driven mergers, the proposed completion of the (English) Channel Tunnel, or the good old American deficit."

According to Professor Wm. C. Freund, the volume of Eurodollars grew from $0.2 trillion in 1972 to $2.5 trillion in 1986. His estimates are much higher than those of Peters chiefly because they include more interbank deposits.

Eurodollars are largely created in the same way as U.S. demand deposits, i.e., by making additional loans in the form of demand deposits. Many of these loans were granted to U.S. borrowers, and, when spent in the U.S., had the same harmful effects as the spending of new demand deposits created by U.S. banks.

All of the arguments I have stated against commercial banking, the private creation of money, in the U.S. apply with equal or greater force to the creation of Eurodollars by foreign banks for use by U.S. firms. Since the volume of Eurodollars is far larger than the volume of bank money created by U.S. banks in the U.S., the danger of inflation due to possible use of Eurodollars in the U.S. may be greater than that due to over creation of U.S. bank money. Indeed, both the world-wide and the U.S. inflation from 1972 to 1981 may have been largely due to the excessive creation of Eurodollars. Therefore, in order to achieve effective control over U.S. price levels, the U.S. will eventually (before 2100) prohibit the creation of such dollars by U.S. banks and their foreign branches, and also prohibit the use of such dollars by U.S. firms and residents.

(5) No Minimum Balances

For many decades, most U.S. commercial banks required that most borrowers maintain minimum compensating balances, usually 20% of any loan, in a demand deposit in the lending bank. And many banks require minimum balances to cover bank operating costs. Such practice not only increased effective interest rates but also distorted data on the quantity of money in use. Any part of a demand deposit which cannot be withdrawn or spent is not a part of the supply of money. Therefore, PCA, the new demand-deposit-holding agency, will not require that depositors maintain compensating bank balances.

Most commercial banks require that small depositors must maintain a minimum balance in order to help the bank cover its costs of operation. The PCA will not require such minimum balances. It will charge service fees high enough to cover its operating costs. The use of service charges is the best way to cover the costs of recording and clearing demand deposit debits and credits because it permits a more accurate allocation of bank costs to those responsible for them. PCA costs will vary with the number of debits and credits, not with the size of the bank balance.

(6) No Overdrafts

The sole reason for requiring that all demand deposits be backed 100% by government paper money is to transfer the power to create new money from commercial banks to a separate government agency. When a commercial bank allows holders of demand deposits to overdraw their deposits, it has created new money which may not show up on bank statements. Therefore, the creation and use of overdraft rights is uneconomic, both because it enables banks to create money and because it may result in false data on the quantity of money.

It may seem that granting reasonable overdraft rights to all demand depositors may reduce the number of bad checks, but there is no good reason to believe that careless depositors will pay more attention to one limit than to another, except perhaps for a short period until depositors become accustomed to the new limit

The ideal way to reduce the number of bad checks and bad EFT orders is to charge penalty fees high enough to achieve the optimum degree of reduction.

However, to assure universal acceptance of checks and EFT orders, the PCA will free all depositors from losses due to bad checks and EFT orders. It will itself recover most such losses by deducting them from future deposits of those who wrote the bad checks and EFT orders. It will cover any net losses by a slight addition to its payment-clearing fees.

4. The Structure and Power of the NMA

The Congress will probably create a National Monetary Authority (NMA) almost completely independent of, and free from, routine direct or indirect control by politicians, bankers, the U.S. Treasury, or any other special interest. If politicians or Treasury officials have any influence over the NMA, they will use it to raise unduly the rate of new money creation in order to increase government revenues and/or reduce taxes. If bankers and debtors have any control, they will use it to lower interest rates.

To make the NMA as independent as possible, the Congress will probably create a control body or commission whose 5 to 7 members serve for life, or for a long fixed term. It will probably also require that all, or at least a majority, of the commission be professional monetary economists, perhaps chosen, or at least approved, by the American Economic Association.

The NMA will be authorized to create all new money and to use at least two methods of putting new money into, and withdrawing it from, circulation:

(1) the purchase and sale of government securities, and (2) the uniform debiting and crediting of all personal (nonbusiness) demand accounts.

The NMA will rely largely, perhaps in time exclusively, on the first method, called open market operations, because this will assure that the elimination of commercial banking does not reduce the supply of liquid capital previously supplied by commercial banks. Moreover, this method will leave the use of such capital up to investors. And open market operations are by far the cheapest method of putting new money into circulation.

The second method, directly debiting and crediting all personal demand accounts, will be used only when the NMA cannot achieve a sufficiently prompt effect on the price level by means of open-market operations. Adjustments in demand deposits can affect the price level much more quickly than can open-market operations because consumers are much more likely to spend additional funds quickly than are investors, who often delay the re-investment of funds.

When adjusting demand deposits, usually upward, the NMA should increase each deposit by the same absolute amount, always in whole dollars. This would benefit most the owners of small deposits, who are most likely to spend new money quickly. Adjustments in round dollars rather than in percentages, would greatly simplify the accounting since no figures in cents would be used.

I believe that, in normal years, the NMA will be able to stabilize the price level by open market operations alone. But it will be authorized to use one or more other, more costly methods, whenever it considers them necessary.

5. The Policies of the NMA

It has been claimed that when the price level for one sector of the economy--agriculture, fuels, etc.--rises or falls sharply, the price level of all goods ought to rise or fall in order to reduce the effect of efforts to stabilize the general price level on the price level of the sector in question. However, any mild general price inflation tends to become runaway inflation. And the government can always help any individual sector of the economy by special measures which do not cause general inflation. Hence, the NMA will be instructed not to cause general inflation in order to help individual sectors, like agriculture.

Many economists have argued that it is often desirable to increase the quantity of money fast enough to cause inflation and widen profit margins in order to prevent or cure a business recession. Unfortunately, beneficial mild inflation too often grows into a harmful runaway inflation which is hard to stop without causing an even more harmful deflation. Therefore, the NMA will be specifically instructed by Congress not to use inflation to prevent or cure business recessions, or to reduce unemployment.

The best way to prevent a business depression is to prevent a decline in the price level, and the best way to cure a mild recession is to restore the price level to its pre-recession level. In both cases, price-level stabilization, not price inflation, is the proper policy.

The best way to reduce unemployment is to provide sufficient vocational education of each kind, and to require large firms to hire all qualified workers at equilibrium wage rates. This will be again elaborated in my next book, <u>Ideal Wages, the Theory of Ideal Wage Rate Determination</u> (1988?).

Every increase in the quantity of loanable funds lowers interest rates, and most new NMA money will probably be used as loan funds, but Congress will instruct the NMA not to create money in order to lower interest rates. Commercial banks have often caused harmful inflation in their efforts to lower interest rates. It is always more socially desirable to stabilize price levels than to lower interest rates by monetary expansion.

Any large change in the quantity of money may affect foreign exchange rates, and central banks have often tried to raise or lower such rates by directly or indirectly increasing or decreasing the rate of creation of bank money, or the quantity of it in circulation. But it is always more desirable to stabilize domestic price levels than to alter foreign exchange rates. Therefore, the U.S. Congress will instruct the NMA to strive only to stabilize domestic price levels, and to ignore the effects of its stabilization measures on foreign exchange rates.

CHAPTER IX. SUMMARY AND FINAL COMMENTS

In this book, I have predicted and discussed six major reforms in our monetary and banking system, all of which will probably be adopted before the year 2100. I shall now briefly restate them, and also review and add up the economic gains which would result from the adoption of these reforms today.

1. Estimates of Gains from Six Reforms

The first major change, the continued further concentration of banking will probably yield significant economies of scale, and significant improvement in services to depositors, but these gains are especially difficult to quantify, and relatively small compared with the gains which will result from other predicted reforms. Therefore, I shall estimate them at zero.

The second coming major reform, the adoption of direct EFT, will radically reduce the costs of making wage payments, sending bills to debtors, and writing checks and mailing them to creditors. About 30 billion checks were used in 1987 to pay personal and commercial bills, to pay wages, and to make other income payments. In Chapter III I estimated the savings to payors and payees, apart from that to banks, at over $1 per check, so the total saving for these checks, as of 1987, would be over $30 billion. The saving in clearing costs for all checks and EFT orders should be over $40 billion.

The third predicted reform, abolition of the creation of bank money, will greatly reduce fluctuations in the level of economic activity and the rate of economic growth. It will probably also increase the average size of our GNP, but it is very difficult to estimate the total dollar value of such benefits, so I make no such estimate here.

The elimination of the creation of money by banks will of course be followed by the formation of a new government agency which will create all new money needed to prevent deflation, and will use its power to stabilize the price level, as forecast in my sixth major prediction. This agency will probably increase the supply of money by 3 to 5% a year, and use the new money to reduce the national debt. This would today reduce the national debt by over $20 billion a year. This is a very conservative estimate because in 1986 U.S. commercial banks, with the aid of the Federal Reserve Banks, actually increased the supply of money by about 15%, which will probably cause the inflation rate to rise above 10% by the end of 1988.

Adoption of my fourth predicted reform, the creation of a single national demand-deposit holding and check-processing agency (PCA) would probably reduce the check-handling costs now incurred by banks by over $1 per check (in 1986 dollars). In 1987, banks processed about 40 billion checks, so the total national saving, as of 1987, is over $40 billion.

The creation of PCA will also permit the U.S. government to appropriate the commercial bank assets created by past creation and loan of bank money, about $100 billion in 1987, which will permit an equal reduction of the national debt. As of 1987, this would have saved the government some $42 billion in interest.

Adoption of my fifth predicted reform, a very great increase in the use of much-improved, comprehensive data on demand-deposit debits and credits to detect crime will probably reduce the costs of crime by over 80%. In 1986 crime cost Americans over $150 billion, so the savings, as of 1987, would be over $700 billion.

The total of these five major economic benefits, as of 1987, comes to about $240 billion, or 5.4% of GNP.

All of these estimates are very rough but they clearly reveal that the adoption of the reforms predicated in this book may yield vast economic benefits to society.

2. Other Predicted Monetary Reforms

In addition to predicting six major reforms, I have also forecast: (1) common use of all automatic teller machines (ATMs), (2) the transfer of all ATMs to PCA, which will standardize them and locate them more rationally, (3) the replacement of most credit cards by a single, nationally-uniform debit card valid in all retail stores, (4) an end to the payment of interest on demand accounts, (5) a ban on checks drawn on time deposits, (6) the elimination of nearly all paper money, and (7) prohibition of the use of Eurodollars in the U.S.

3. The Rationalization of Other Service Industries

Many futurists have predicted that the service sector of the U.S. economy will continue to grow faster than the commodity-production sector. They seem to be unaware of the immense possible savings which will be achieved by future rationalization of most large service industries. For instance, the real costs of commercial banking, insurance, security brokerage, real estate brokerage, legal and judicial services, crime protection, and entertainment could be reduced by 50 to 80% by reorganizing these industries.

(1) Rationalizing the Security Brokerage Industry

The transfer of securities from one U.S. investor to another now usually involves a compensating transfer of demand deposits, and, as predicted in Chapter VII, the use of cash to purchase securities will soon become illegal. Most of the arguments for concentrating all transfers of demand accounts in a single national office can be used to justify a like concentration of all security transfers. It is just as wasteful to spend money on transporting securities from one brokerage office to another as to spend money on transporting checks from one bank to another. Therefore, in time a single national security brokerage agency which holds, and transfers titles to, all securities will be created, probably before the year 2100 A.D. The prices paid will probably be determined automatically by a computer complex programmed to fix prices which balance supply and demand.

Since every security transfer will involve a compensating transfer of demand deposits, and should not be carried out unless the required demand deposits are available, the national security agency should be very closely associated, both organizationally and geographically, with the national demand-deposit transfer agency. Probably these two functions will be performed by the same computer complex in a single building, and both security and demand-deposit holdings and transfers will be reported on the same periodic statements.

The creation of this national brokerage monopoly will eliminate all need for local brokerage offices. Orders to buy and sell securities will be mailed or phoned to the national brokerage agency. Ample advice on the purchase or sale of securities will be provided by investment periodicals and books. The elimination of local brokerage offices will save over $10 billion a year.

The deposit of all securities in the vaults of a single national brokerage agency will not only save the high costs of locating, counting, verifying, and transporting these securities whenever they are transferred from one owner to another, but will also greatly reduce both storage costs and losses from thefts, embezzlement, and fire. If anyone tries to sell securities he does not own, the national brokerage agency will find it easy to detect his illegal effort, or to reverse the sale after it has been found to be illegal. No seller will be paid in cash, and illegal demand-deposit payments will be easily reversible. Moreover, no sale will be completed unless the buyer has adequate funds in his demand account, which will be held by the affiliated national check-handling agency. Finally, concentrating all security brokerage in a single national agency will create an ideal market by bringing all buyers and sellers together in a single perfect 24-hour a day market for the first time.

(2) Rationalizing the Insurance Industry

The insurance industry also will soon be radically reformed and rationalized in ways similar to those I have predicted for the commercial banking and brokerage industries.

In an advanced country every adult should be guaranteed an ideal amount of income, health, and property insurance, whether or not he asks for it. In other words, such insurance coverage should be universal and compulsory because it will benefit both the individual and society.

To achieve this goal at a minimum cost, the U.S. government will reform and rationalize the insurance industry. It will eliminate the need for insurance salesmen and advertising by making insurance compulsory. It will radically reduce the cost of collecting insurance premiums by making payment compulsory and by using direct EFT to collect them. It will sharply reduce other operating costs by merging all insurance firms into a single firm, and thereby make possible many more economies of large-scale operation and management. The new national insurance agency (NIA) will be located very close to the PCA in order to minimize the cost and time required to debit and credit billions of individual demand deposits held by PCA.

The essential function of an insurance firm is to collect billions of dollars by debiting millions of demand accounts, and to pay millions of insurance benefits by crediting such accounts. If the NIA is located next to the PCA, the costs of transmitting debit and credit orders to the PCA will be minimized. NIA will then need local offices around the country only to house insurance adjusters who verify claims for property loss and damage. These rationalization measures will be adopted before 2100 A.D. in the U.S., and will reduce insurance operating costs per dollar of benefits by over 60%. At present, the operating costs of private insurance companies amount to over 30% of total benefits paid, while such costs are less than 5% of social security benefits.

Banking, brokerage, and insurance are large service industries. If my prediction that rationalization of these industries will reduce employment in them by 60-80% is correct, the common belief that service industries will grow much faster than manufacturing industries is suspect. Many other service industries--health care, real estate brokerage, advertising, accounting, tax and investment counseling, automobile retailing, gasoline retailing, etc.--can easily be reformed so as to reduce employment in them by over 50%. For instance, U.K. health costs amount to only 5% of GNP, while U.S. health costs amount to over 11% of GNP, with similar death rates.

4. More Criticism of the Service Industry Thesis

The above comments on the rationalization of service industries cast doubt on the common claim that employment in service industries will long continue to grow faster than employment in commodity-producing industries. I have another criticism of this theory. If the work performed by service-industry workers is very similar to the work done by workers in non-service industries, the theory that service industries are growing, and will continue to grow, faster than other industries is much less informative and significant than its proponents claim it to be. I believe that the work done by a great many, perhaps most, service providers is very similar to the work done by other workers.

There are two main classes of service industries, those which provide personal services—education, health care, etc.—and those which provide impersonal or mechanical services—public utilities, transport, etc. The work done by personal-service workers does differ radically from that done by workers producing commodities, but the work done by providers of impersonal services does not. In fact, it is very similar. For instance, most public utility and railroad workers construct and maintain physical facilities, or tend machines, or purchase and store raw materials and equipment, or perform other tasks very similar to those done by workers in commodity-producing industries. The air transport industry, a major new service industry, employs thousands of mechanics who keep aircraft in working order. Their work differs little from that of workers in aircraft factories.

5. Other Comments

Nearly all of the six major monetary and banking reforms predicted above will occur gradually and simultaneously over several decades. Only the creation of a single national demand-deposit holding and payment-clearing agency will probably require a sudden drastic compulsory change in the system. And even this radical reform can be largely achieved gradually and without government coercion if free competition results in the survival of only one national chain of commercial banks.

All of the predicted reforms, and many others, will be aspects or illustrations of a much more general or fundamental social trend, namely the universal and inevitable trend towards rationalization of all economic behavior. Mankind has an instinctive or hereditary desire to rationalize, or make efficient, all social behavior. Thus it is always possible to predict the future by determining what behavior will be most rational or efficient.

Most major social trends have been, and will long continue to be similar in all advanced countries. I am therefore confident that the predictions I have made concerning major future trends and events in money and banking in the U.S. also apply to other advanced countries. For instance, I feel sure that Japan, the U.K., France, Germany, and other equally advanced countries will abolish commercial banking, concentrate all demand deposits in national payment-clearing monopolies, prohibit all large payments in cash, and use payment data as a major method of crime detection before the year 2100.

Many recent writers of texts on economics, money, and money and banking have ignored proposed reforms like 100% money because they believe that they are now politically unacceptable. But nearly all major social and economic reforms were considered to be politically unacceptable 50 years before they were adopted. For instance, guarantee of bank deposits was unacceptable 50 years before it was adopted, and was therefore little discussed in 1880 economic textbooks. But any thoughtful forward-looking 1880 economist could understand the strong case for such a guarantee. This implies that it is possible to predict the future by predicting that desirable reforms will be adopted. I believe that all economic texts should explain why such reforms are coming, whether or not they are now politically acceptable. Adoption of this policy will both speed up the process of social reform and result in more intelligent design of desirable reforms.

BIBLIOGRAPHY

* These texts ignore the social utility of commercial banking, forced saving, 100% money, and EFT, except as noted here or earlier.

Anon, "Atlanta Study..." Econ. R., Fed. Res. Bk of Atlanta, June, 1981.
Adams, John, Works, 1854 ed., p. 375.
Anderson, B.M., "Bank Money and the Capital Supply," Chase Econ. Bul., V1,3.
Anderson, Jack, "Electronic Bank Panic," S.F. Chronicle, 5-20-87, p. 83.
*Auerbach, R.D., M. B., and Fin. Markets, 2nd ed., (1985), Mentions EFT (p. 13) and 100% money (p. 575).

*Bach, G.L., Economics... 6th ed., (1968).
*Barro, R.J., Macroeconomics, (1984).
*Baxter, Wm. F., et al, Retail Banking in the Electronic Age (1977).
Beckwith, B.P., Contemporary...Theories [of] the Effect of Com. Bank. on the Supply of Physical Capital, (1935).
Behravesh, N., see Mansfield
Bender, M.G., EFTS... (1975), p. 11.
Bennett, V.M., "Check Safekeeping," Econ. R., FRBA, Oct. '82.
Berger, A.N., and D.B. Humphrey, "The Role of Interstate Banking in the Diffusion of EFT," in Colin and Shay, Technological Innovation... (1986).
Bollman, E., Paragraphs on Banks, 2nd ed., (1811).
Boorman, J.T. and T.M., Money Supply... (1972).
*Boughton, J.M., et al, The Prin. of Monetary Econ. (1975).
*Bradley, M., "Macroeconomics" 2nd ed., (1985).
*Brockway, G.P., Economics... (1985).
*Burstein, M.L., Money (1963).

Cannan, Edwin, An Economist's Protest (1927), pp.224-5
Carey, H.C., Money, (1857), pp. 26-27.
*Chandler, L.V., Econ. of M and B., 4th ed. (1964).
Cooper, Thomas, Lectures on the Elements of P.E. (1826), pp. 37-38.
*Crump, T., The Phenom. of Money (1981), p. 146.
*Culbertson, J.M., Money and B., (1972). Mentions 100% money.

Dorfman, J., The Econ. Mind., III, pp. 422-23.
Dornburg, Thomas, Macroeconomics... 7th ed., (1985).
*Dow, S.C., and P.E. Earl, Money Matters... (1982).
Dunbar, C.F., The Theory and History of Banking, 5th ed., (1929).

Ferris, J.A., The Fin. Econ. of the U.S.... (1867).
*Fisher, D., M and B. (1971).
Fisher, Irving, 100% Money (1935).
———. The Purchasing Power of Money (1911).
Flannery, M.J. and D.W. Jaffe, The Economic Implications of an EMTS (1973).
Frazer, P., Plastic and Electronic Money... (1985).
Friday, D., Profits, Wages & Prices (1921).
Friedman, Milton, A Program for Mon. Stability (1960).

*Galbraith, J.K., Money... (1975).
*Godley, W., and F. Cripps, Macroeconomics (1983).
*Goldfield, S.M., and L.V. Chandler, The Econ. of M. and B., 8th ed., (1981)
Gouge, W.M., The Journal of Banking... (1842).
*Greenway, D. and D.K. Shaw, Macroeconomics... (1983).
Greenspan, Alan, "March Interview..." S.F. Chron. (6-9-87), p. 56.

*Hall, R.E., and J.B. Taylor, Macroeconmics (1986).
Hamilton, Alexander, Writings, III, p. 394.
Hansen, A.H., Business Cycle Theory (1927).
*Harrod, Roy, Money (1969).
Hempel, G.H., Bank Management... 2nd ed., (1986).
*Hendrickson, R.A., The Cashless Society (1972).
*Henin, P., Macrodynamics... (1986).
Hentzka, Theodore, Freeland, (1891).
Hopton, D., Payment Systems... (1983).
Horner, F., "An Inquiry... Edinburgh R., I (1802), pp. 172-201.
Horvitz, P.M., "Techno. Innovation...Fin. Institutions," in Lawrence and Shay, op. cit.
*Hosek, Wm. R., and F. Zahn, Monetary Theory... (1977).
Humes, K.H., "The Checkless-Cashless Society... Futurist, Oct., 1978.

Jaffe, D.W., see Flannery
Jefferson, Thomas, The Writings of... (1904), XIII, p. 407.
Johnson, A.B., "A Treatise on B." Bankers Mag. III (1840), p. 736.

*Kamerschen, D.R., and E.S. Klise, M and B, 6th ed. (1976). Discussses 100% money.

*Kaufman, G.G., Money, the Fin. System & the Econ., 3rd ed., (1981). Has 2 pp. on EFT.
*Kent, R.P., M and B, 5th ed., (1966), pp. 112-13.
*Kettle, B., Monetary Econ. (1985).
Kleene, J.F., "Productive Apparatus & the Capitalist," J. of Pol. Econ., Feb., 1923.
*Klein, J.J., Money... 6th ed., (1986).

Laughlin, J.L., The Prin. of Money (1903), pp. 85-86.
Lawrence, C., and R.P. Shay, Techno. Innova., Regula., and the Mon. Econ. (1986).
LeKachman, R.L., "The Debt Balloon," Dissent, Spring, 1876.
Leman, N., "Change in the Banks," Atlantic M., Aug., 1985.
Lipis, A.H., et al, Electronic Banking (1985).
*Luckett, D.G., Money and B., (1976), p. 143.
*Ludtke, J.B., Am. Fin. System, 2d ed., (1967).

Malthus, R., "Publica. on the Deprecia. of Paper Currency," The Edinburgh R., XVII, pp. 340-72.
*Mansfield, E., and N. Behravesh, Economics, USA, (1986) p. 169.
*Marshall, B.V., Comprehen. Economics... 2nd ed., (1973).
Mayer, Martin, The Money Bazaars, (1984).
*Mayer, T., et al, M., B., and the Econ. (1981).
Mill, James, Elem. of P.E., 3rd ed., (1826).
Mill, John S. Prin. of P.E., rev. ed., (1900).
Miller, H.E., Banking Theory in the U.S. before 1860, (1925), 103n.
*Moore, B.J., An Intro. to Modern Econ. Theory (1973).
Morone, Wm.R., "NACHA's Future Rule," ER, FRBA, April, 1986
Moulton, H.G., "Com. Banking and Capital Forma." J. of Pol. Econ., XXVI (1918), 484-508, 638-63, 705-31, 849-81.

Newton, Max., The Fed (1983).
*Nichols, D.A., and C.W. Reynolds, Prin. of Econ., (1971).

Osterberg, R., "POS is on its Way," ER, FRBA, July, 1984.

*Peach, W.M., Prin. of Econ. (1963).
*Prather, C.L., Money and B., 8th ed., (1965).
*Prescott, P.B., Money, B., and Econ. Welfare (1960).

Rae, John, The Sociolog. Theory of Capital... (1834).

Raguet, C., A Treatise on Currency & Banking, 2nd ed., (1840), pp. 86, 158.
*Rasmussen, D.W., and C.I. Haworth, Economics (1979).
Raymond, Daniel, Elements of P.E., 2nd ed., 1836.
*Revell, J.R.S., Banking and Electronic Fund Transfers (1983).
Ricardo, D., The Prin. of P.E. and Taxation (1817).
Richardson, D.W., Electronic Money... (1970).
Ritter, L.S. and W.L. Silver, Prin. of M, B, and Fin. Markets, 5th ed., (1984).
*Robinson, J., and J. Eatwell, Intro. to Mod. Econ., (1973).
Rothbard, M.N., The Mystery of Banking (19 3).

*Samuelson, P., and W.D. Nordhaus, Economics, 12th ed., (1986).
*Schiller, B.R., The Macroeconomy Today (1980).
*Shapiro, Edw., Understanding Money, (1975).
*Simpson, T.D., Money, B., and Econ. Anal., 3rd ed., 1987.
Smith, Adam, The Wealth of Nations (1776), p. 257.
*Smith, Harlan M., The Essentials of Money and Banking (1968). Has 2 pp. discus. of 100% money.
Sprague, O.M.W., 5th ed. of Dunbar, p. 95.
Spulber, N., The Soviet Econ. (1966).
Statistical Abstract of the U.S.
Stewart, Dugald, Collected Works (1855).
Stone, B.K., "Electronic Payments..." Econ. R., FRBA, Mar. 1986, p. 29.

Taussig, F.W., Prin. of Econ. (1911), p. 17.
Taylor, John, An Inquiry into... (1814).
*Thomas, L.B., Jr., M, B, and Econ. Activity, 3rd ed., (1986). Has 3 pp. on EFT.
Thompson, R.E., "A Treatise on B," Bankers' Mag. III (1849).
*Thomson, F.P., Money in the Computer Age (1968).
*Thorn, R.S., Intro. to M and B (1976).
*Timberlake, R.H., and E. B. Selby, Money and B, (1972). Contains good 7 pages on 100% money.
Tucker, George, The Theory of Money... (1839), p. 181.

*Vane, H.R., and J.L. Thompson, An Intro. to Macroecon. Policy (1985).
*Vickers, D., M, B, and the Macroeconomy, (1985).

Wachtel, H., The Money Mandarins (1985).
Walker, Amasa, The Science of Wealth... 4th ed. (1872).
Waldron, D., and L.D. Ball, "The Bottom Line on Checkless Banking." Technology R, Feb., 1980.

INDEX

ABOUT THE AUTHOR

Born in Carthage, Missouri, in 1904, and raised largely in Pasadena, California, Burnham Putnam Beckwith was graduated from Stanford University with a B.A. in Philosophy in 1926. He spent the next two years at the Harvard Business School, and, after three more years of full-time graduate study, received a Ph.D. in economics from the University of Southern California in 1932. He held a post-doctoral research-training assistantship under Dr. Edward L. Thorndike at Teachers' College, Columbia University, from 1935 to 1937. He also taught economics at the University of Kansas, Queens College (NYC), and the University of Georgia before going to work for the War Production Board (D.C.) in 1941. From 1945 to 1948 he worked for the War Department in France (Biarritz American University) and in Germany (OMGUS, Berlin).

Since 1948 he has devoted all his time to writing books and articles on philosophy, religion, socialist economic theory, futurism, and social reform. His books include _Religion, Philosophy, and Science, an Introduction to Logical Positivism_ (1956), _The Next 500 Years, Scientific Predictions of Major Social Trends_ (1967), _Liberal Socialism_ (1974), _Government by Experts, the Next State in Political Evolution_ (1972), _Free Goods_ (1976), _Ideas About the Future_ (2nd ed., 1986), and _Beyond Tomorrow, a Rational Utopia_ (1986). He has also published articles in _Dissent_, _The Humanist_, _Free Inquiry_, and _The Futurist_.